*There are two things of
lasting value we can give
our children - one is roots,
the other is wings.*

—Anonymous

STARTING YOUNG ᔅᴹ

Supporting Parents for
Peaceful Lifestyles

activities to promote social
and emotional development
in children from
birth to three years

A project developed by:
• Peace Links
• Family Foundations Early Head Start of the Office of
  Child Development, University of Pittsburgh

Emie Tittnich, M.S.
Project Developer

Major funding for this project was provided by:
Alcoa Foundation

Additional funding from: BridgeBuilders Foundation

Matinicus Press

Peace Links

i

STARTING YOUNG^{SM}

ISBN 0-9765689-0-X

Published by Matinicus Press
734 Cleveland Avenue
Brackenridge, PA 15014

Printed in the United States of America.

*If we are to have real
peace in the world,
we shall have to begin
with the children.*
—Gandhi

STARTING YOUNG^{SM}

Table of Contents

sowing seeds of peace

Where, after all, do universal human rights begin?
In all places, close to home, so close and so small
That they cannot be seen on any maps of the world.
Unless these rights have meaning there,
They have little meaning anywhere.
-Eleanor Roosevelt

STARTING YOUNGSM is dedicated to helping children become securely attached to parents and caregivers and to establishing peaceful lifestyles in their daily lives. It was developed within a partnership forged between Pennsylvania Peace Links and Family Foundations Early Head Start, a program of the University of Pittsburgh's Office of Child Development.

Children begin to understand concepts of peace and justice when they have a firm sense of trust: trust that others will keep them safe; trust that they can have an effect on their world; and trust that they will have all that they need (perhaps not all that they want, but all that they need). **STARTING YOUNG**SM seeks to funnel those lofty ideals down to their "close, small places" - relationships between parents and young children.

The Activities in this publication are designed for caregivers including home visitors, family and child development specialists, early childhood educators, and others who work in partnership with parents. Created for infants and toddlers, the activities are built around seven social and emotional development goals that foster positive, healthy growth. They lend themselves to a relationship-based approach to working with young children and their families. The conversational tone and suggested language are intended to set the stage for an interactional style that fosters relationships with the child.

Recent neurobiological research in human development emphasizes early childhood as critical to a child's understanding of the world and the course of growth across the lifespan. We know now that the environment, experiences, and relationships have the power to greatly impact a young child's development and learning, beginning at birth.

The **STARTING YOUNG**SM Project is committed to helping caregivers raise their children based on their families' strengths. It is also designed to encourage families to take pride and pleasure in their children.

The project grew out of concerns about interpersonal and societal aggression. The escalating effects of war, terrorism, and violence, including school violence, bullying, and intimidation, heightened our concerns. We believe that supporting parents for peaceful lifestyles early in the parent-child relationship will help to reduce stress and conflict in the first years. We further contend that it is possible to break the cycles of hostility and aggression by instilling, at an early age, the message that conflict can be resolved in peaceful ways.

We believe that, in the words of Alcoa Foundation which supported this project from the beginning, "Sometimes parents need training and support from caring community services to fulfill (their) critical responsibility," and that by "beginning with the children" we are upholding Peace Links' mission to lessen conflict and promote international understanding.

acknowledgements

Alcoa Foundation's affirmation of the partnership between Pennsylvania Peace Links and Family Foundations Early Head Start helped it grow beyond our original concept. We are very grateful to Kathleen W. Buechel, President of the Foundation, N. Lucy Keith and Evelyn Whitehill, Program Officers for this project, and Innocenzio A. Grignano, consultant.

Alcoa Foundation President Kathleen W. Buechel understood, long before others, the underlying significance of "Starting Young" in the care and education of our very youngest members of society. After its lead grant in 1997, Alcoa Foundation continued, with additional funding, to support its belief that parents are their children's first teachers and that early support for a child's healthy development lays the foundation for positive social and emotional growth.

The Peace Links' committee is made up of professional early childhood educators, psychologists, and a pioneer in the prevention of child abuse. The work was born out of Peace Links' early initiatives that created programs in conflict management for young children. From its investigations and requests by early childhood educators and caregivers came the determination to focus on the youngest members of the human community, those from birth to three. Hence, the **STARTING YOUNG** project took form. The committee, chaired by Evelyn Murrin, Ed.M., C.A.S., was comprised of: Elizabeth Elmer, M.S.S., co-chair; June Delano, Ph.D.; Winifred Feise, M.S.; Margaret F. McCoy, B.A., M. Litt.; Cary Peterson, B.S.; Miki Rakay, M.Ed.; Adelaide Smith, M.P.A.; Margaret Tauxe, M.A.; and Elsa Zollars, M.Ed. Technical assistance was provided by Anne Kuhn, with the guidance and editing services rendered by Lois Goldstein, M.Ed. and Barbara Myers, M.Ed. Mary Vallejo consulted with the Committee about adoptions and wrote "Toddler Adoption" for the new Difficult Situations section. Special thanks to Janice Auth, Executive Director of Peace Links.

Peace Links' partnership with Family Foundations Early Head Start at the University of Pittsburgh began in 1996. We were inspired by the leadership of Laurie Mulvey, M.S.W., Director of Service Demonstrations, Office of Child Development, University of Pittsburgh, who served as an early advisor to this project. Throughout our collaboration, the vision of Vivian Herman, M.S.W., Project Director, Family Foundations Early Head Start, and her steadfast beliefs in early relationship building between parent and child, as well as working from a family's strengths, led us to appreciate the promise, for children, of those perspectives. Child Development Specialist Emie Tittnich, M.S., brought her knowledge of infants and toddlers, which deepened the work, and her association with Early Head Start staff gave us the family stories and situations upon which the activities were designed.

We are indebted to all of the Family Foundations Early Head Start staff, past and present, who field tested the activities in their work with the families they serve in McKees Rocks, Clairton, and Terrace Village (now Oak Hill). Thanks also to Anna Whalen and the staff of the Homewood Brushton Family Support Center. The following staff gave written reviews of the activities: Jennifer Curuso and the staff of Family Foundations McKees Rocks, and Chris Dunkerley, Family Foundations Clairton. In addition, April Belsky, a parent from Clairton Family Foundations, reviewed the activities.

A special thanks to Franzetta Wilborn and Jeffrey Burton, Family Foundations, who gave guidance to the project with regard to the "Memory Book-Establishing Family Treasures" activity. This activity was made possible by funding provided by BridgeBuilders Foundation, The Urban Affairs Foundation of the United Jewish Federation, Giant Eagle inc., Target Stores, Inc. and Konica.

We are grateful to the community agencies that reviewed the activities for relevance to their work with families: Pam Long, Allegheny County Health Department, Maternal and Child Health division; Carole Stangle, Infant-Toddler Teacher for Valley Community Services Child Care; and Janet Crawford, Children's Hospital Community Education Program.

Reed Smith, LLP provided *pro-bono* legal assistance in all intellectual property matters. We thank them for their generosity.

The project was carried out during the tenures of Peace Links' presidents Adelaide Smith, Lois Goldstein, and Anne Kuhn, whose leadership, along with the encouragement of the entire board, sustained our belief that in order to fulfill Peace Links' mission, we must, as Gandhi urged "Begin with the Children".

the first edition

The first edition of this book has been successfully used by caregivers and others who help families of young children. We appreciate the thoughtful evaluations of those who used the first edition. They report that it is the only book that deals with issues of violence prevention, that promotes parent-child interaction, and focuses on activities for social and emotional development. "For many families, violence in their daily environments is a reality (whether it is at home or in the neighborhood) and this book addresses those issues and can be used to open the conversation with parents."

After studying formal evaluations and suggestions from focus groups following the first edition of **STARTING YOUNG** and encouraged by its users, Peace Links embarked on a marketing survey and strategy for its wider distribution. Peace Links is grateful to Mr. and Mrs. C.J. Witting for their financial support of the feasibility and planning study conducted by Michele Q. Margittai.

---

the new edition

This new edition of **STARTING YOUNG** offers a new format, including:

- an easy-to-use design
- illustrations by pre-school children
- a glossary of terms
- an additional section which addresses "Difficult Situations" in parenting

Thank you to BridgeBuilders Foundation for their funding of this publication.

We are fortunate to have a unique design, created by Professor Daniel Boyarski, Professor and Head of the School of Design at Carnegie Mellon University. His *pro-bono* contributions make this version easier to navigate and visually more interesting. The sections titled "Developmental Teaching" and "Developmental Information" distinguish **STARTING YOUNG**. In Professor Boyarsky's design, those sections are now prominent and easily accessible.

Children at the Arsenal Family and Children's Center, Carlow University Child Care and Preschool Centers, the Carnegie Mellon University Children's School, The Cyert Early Childhood Center at Carnegie Mellon University, and the Little Angels Day Care Center prepared the illustrations found throughout the book. We appreciate their willingness to share their emerging artistic talents.

Evelyn Murrin, Chair
Peace Links **STARTING YOUNG** Committee
"Begin With the Children" Programs

description of goals

The social and emotional goals for this project are designed for young children in the first three years of their life.

1. THE CHILD WILL DEVELOP A SENSE OF BODY SELF AND SELF-REGULATION.
During the early months of life, infants develop a pattern of eating, sleeping, and other biological functions. This self-scheduling is an important first step in the infant's ability to calm herself, and later in development to have control over impulses. As babies experience discomfort, they look to an outside source to make them feel better. Over time, they learn to give a sign to the caregiver that they are hungry, wet, or need to be held close. When caregivers change discomfort to pleasure by feeding, diapering, or holding, babies develop trust that their needs will be met, and they start to form a close relationship with the person who provides the comfort.

Having needs consistently met gives baby a sense of predictability, setting the stage for learning the concept of time. Holding and other physical interaction, making eye contact and sharing pleasurable activities sets the stage for babies' learning about themselves as being separate from caregivers. They learn about body boundaries, theirs and others.

2. THE CHILD WILL DEVELOP AN UNDERSTANDING OF HOW THINGS WORK AND HOW TO MAKE THINGS HAPPEN.
In the first few months of life, babies make many movements and some of these produce results. For example, the mobile makes a sound or moves after the baby kicks it. This is the beginning of learning about cause and effect or consequences of actions. This curiosity about the world can only evolve if basic needs for food and comfort are met. As the child grows and can walk and manipulate objects, she learns that she can cause things to drop, to move, etc., and that she can have some control over her environment.

3. THE CHILD WILL DEVELOP TRUST THROUGH SECURE ATTACHMENTS AND MEANINGFUL RELATIONSHIPS.
When needs are met consistently, babies become aware of changes from discomfort to comfort and they turn their attention to the source of that comfort. They create a mental map of that person, the face, the smell, and even the taste of that person. They associate that person, the mental image, with the good feelings of comfort and make an attachment. It is important that the care be provided by a limited number of adults so baby's mental image can grow sharper with each interaction with the caregiver. Baby will view this caregiver as special and will want to please her. That sets the stage for compliance, socialization, and self-control. Once the attachment is made, the baby's task over the next three years is to move to separate, to feel comfortable managing some things, to become independent, and to become confident in the ability to get things done.

4. **THE CHILD WILL DEVELOP THE ABILITY TO EXPRESS FEELINGS IN APPROPRIATE WAYS.**

Shortly after birth, when babies feel uncomfortable they can become fearful, feeling that their discomfort will persist. They sometimes become angry. Once babies experience predictable patterns of caregiving, they are able to control their anger. They might feel angry, but they do not act on those feelings. When they experience pleasure in their interactions with adults, they act in pleasurable ways. Sometime during the middle of the first year, babies begin to mirror the emotions shown by their parents. It is important to allow children to feel the full range of joy and anger, sadness and contentment, among others.

5. **THE CHILD WILL DEVELOP THE ABILITY TO FOLLOW DIRECTIONS AND ACCEPT LIMITS.**

When babies can predict that their needs will be met and they trust that comfort is coming, they are willing to wait awhile for needs to be satisfied. With trust in the caregiver and assurance of getting what they need, babies can stop themselves from crying in rage, or later, acting out to get someone to care for them.

6. **THE CHILD WILL DEVELOP THE ABILITY TO PLAY, PRETEND, AND USE SYMBOLS.**

Once babies are sure that their needs will be met, they use their remaining energy for play and learning. As parents talk to children about objects, events, actions, and reactions, the babies learn that there are labels for all of these feelings. Babies create mental images not only of important people, such as mother, but also of objects and names for them. Later, they can use the name to refer to the object, even when the object is not present. This ability to use language to refer to things not currently present, or events not currently happening, is the beginning of symbolization.

7. **THE CHILD WILL DEVELOP THE ABILITY TO BE A MUTUALLY RESPONSIVE PARTNER AND ENGAGE IN PRO-SOCIAL BEHAVIOR.**

When attachments are strong, babies and young children will identify with the standards of the parents. They act in the same way the parent does. They respond to others as others have responded to them. If those actions have been gentle and caring, children will learn to show gentleness and caring to others. If children have not been treated respectfully, with gentleness, they will respond the same way to others. When parents are intolerant of their children's imitative behavior and try to change that behavior, the child feels powerless. An example of this is stopping the child from hitting the adult. If the child continues to experience an adult's aggression, that child might use other children as the object of its frustrated powerlessness, and in turn, become aggressive.

Adapted from Landy, S. and DeV.Peters, Ray (1991), "Understanding and Treating the Hyperaggressive Toddler," *Zero to Three*, February, pp 22-31

glossary

AUTONOMY   The state of independence, of being able to act alone

BODY SELF   Knowledge of physical self; an image or idea about one's physical being

BOUNDARIES   Knowledge of limits, both physical and social/emotional

CAREGIVER   A person who cares for children in a specific environment designed for the healthy, safe growth of young children

COGNITIVE   Having to do with the mind, thinking

DEVELOPMENTAL INFORMATION   Knowledge that relates to a specific age of childhood

DEVELOPMENTAL TASKS   Activities or behaviors that are expected at certain ages: infancy, toddlers, preschoolers, kindergarten, etc. and which lay the foundations for accomplishing the next developmental tasks

DEVELOPMENTAL TEACHING   Teaching that is appropriate for specific ages of childhood

EMPATHY   Recognition of another's feelings or state of being. The capacity to feel what another person is feeling

HOME VISITOR   A person trained to work with parents of young children in the home

IDENTITY   The knowledge of self, who I am

IMPULSE-CONTROL   The ability to contain the desire to act immediately in response to an urge

INDIRECT APPEALS   Nonverbal requests, using facial expressions, sounds, and /or hand and body movements

MENTAL IMAGE   A picture one has in one's head; mental map

MUTUALLY RESPONSIVE BEHAVIOR   Understanding what is required and acting on it without the use of language

NON-VERBAL COMMUNICATION   Expressing needs without the use of words

OBJECT PERMANENCE   The ability to remember something when it is out of sight, no longer in view

PRO-SOCIAL BEHAVIOR   Behavior that is appropriate for children of a given age; behavior that is appropriate in a family or group of children and which helps to solve problems

SELF-REGULATION   Control of one's body functions and behaviors

SENSORY   Dealing with seeing, hearing, touching, smelling, and tasting

SYMBOLIZATION   The ability to represent ideas or things with objects or crafts such as a block or a pretend telephone

TRANSITIONAL OBJECT   A familiar beloved item that is comforting and will help a child link a familiar place to a new, unfamiliar place i.e., a blanket, teddy bear, mother's scarf

UPRIGHT MOBILITY   The ability to stand on two feet and to move and play in this position

organization of activities

The Peace Links **STARTING YOUNG** Activities are designed to be used with young children and their families. Parents can easily adapt them for their own use. The activities are categorized by age, using the ages from birth – 12 months, 12 – 24 months, and 24 – 36 months. Some of the activities are designed to be used over multiple age categories. With some creativity and imagination, many of the activities can be adapted for older or younger children. Each age section includes an index of activities listed for that age category.

Within each age category the activities are further divided by goals. These seven goals (adapted from Landy and DeV. Peters, 1991) are listed here and described on pages xi and xii. Table I lists the goals. Table II, on page xvi, lists the activities by age for each goal, and their corresponding page numbers.

Table 1

Goal Number	Goal Title
1	The child will develop a sense of self and self-regulation.
2	The child will develop an understanding of how things work and how to make things happen.
3	The child will develop trust through secure attachments and meaningful relationships.
4	The child will develop the ability to express feelings in appropriate ways.
5	The child will develop the ability to follow directions and accept limits.
6	The child will develop the ability to play, pretend and use symbols.
7	The child will develop the ability to be a responsive partner and engage in pro-social behavior.

How to Use the Activities

The activities are designed to be easy to use. Refer to the age category that reflects the age of the child for whom the activity is intended. Select an activity, read it over, and make any modifications that might be needed for the child.

Table II
Goals and Activities by Child Age

Activity	Title	Child Age in Months			Page Number
		0-12	12-24	24-36	
Goal 1	**THE CHILD WILL DEVELOP A SENSE OF BODY SELF AND SELF-REGULATION.**				
	Goodnight Moon	x	x	x	3
	Me and My Body	x	x	x	5
	Stop and Go	x	x		7
	Mirror, Mirror	x	x		9
	Fingers and Toes	x	x		11
	Conversations: Now You are One		x		63
	Conversations: Now You are Two			x	97
	Conversations: Now You are Three			x	107
Goal 2	**THE CHILD WILL DEVELOP AN UNDERSTANDING OF HOW THINGS WORK AND HOW TO MAKE THINGS HAPPEN.**				
	My Turn, Your Turn	x			13
	Please Mother	x	x		15
	Lunchtime	x			17
	Shake, Rattle and Roll	x	x		19
	Coffee Can Drop		x	x	67
	Cooking Eggs		x	x	69
	Changes in Our Lives			x	99
Goal 3	**THE CHILD WILL DEVELOP TRUST THROUGH SECURE ATTACHMENTS AND MEANINGFUL RELATIONSHIPS.**				
	A Rose by any Other Name	x			21
	Conversations: Before You Came	x			23
	Praise Phrases	x	x	x	25
	Journals: How You've Grown	x	x	x	27
	Conversations: When You Were a Baby	x			29
	Memory Book	x	x	x	31
	Leaving	x			33
	Toy Toss		x	x	71
	Places in the Heart		x	x	73
	Letting Go			x	101
Goal 4	**THE CHILD WILL DEVELOP THE ABILITY TO EXPRESS FEELINGS IN APPROPRIATE WAYS.**				
	Let's Read	x	x	x	35
	Let's Dance	x	x	x	37
	Let's Sing	x	x	x	39
	What's Inside		x	x	75
	Tearing Paper			x	103
	Make it Bite			x	105
	Hold Me			x	109
	My Way			x	111

Index to Activities: Birth–12 months

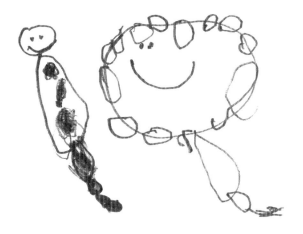

Goodnight Moon

I will write peace
on your wings
and you will fly
all over the world.

—Sadako Sasaki

GOAL The child will develop a sense of body self and self-regulation.

AGE Birth to 36 months

PURPOSE To provide the opportunity to talk about separations. This activity will give an opening to talk with parents about rituals associated with bedtime and other types of separations. It can also develop competence around literacy.

STORY THEME

Bedtime rituals, Separations

STORY SYNOPSIS

At the end of the day the child is put to bed in a room full of meaningful objects. The child says "Good night" to these familiar things.

DISCUSSING THE STORY

Encourage the mother to read the story to her baby at bedtime. There is a board book available and the story is short. The story can be read to infants, or the mother and baby can look at the pictures together and name the objects. When objects are similar to those the baby might have, the mother should acknowledge that, using baby's name (e.g., "Jason has a ball just like that one.") The mother should read the story on several consecutive days, referring to the last time the story was read. Engage the mother in a discussion of the importance of reading the story. Ask her to share meaningful stories from her childhood and discuss why the story is appealing. Encourage the mother to tell as well as read stories to the baby. Literacy development is supported by reading a story and then conducting story-related activities. Encourage the mother to do one or more of the following when it is appropriate to the age of the child.

STORY-RELATED ACTIVITIES

Photos Take a picture of the mother reading the book to her baby. Have her write or dictate her feelings about her baby and/or the activity.

I Like You Have the mother record something positive about her baby's characteristics, such as, "I like the way your nose wrinkles when you yawn." Suggest that the mother write her comments between home-visits, maybe one every day, or every other day, as time permits. These could be read to the baby and saved for him to read when he is able.

Bedtime routine Help the mother select 2 to 3 activities that are routinely done before bedtime. Help her identify a transition object or a meaningful toy for her baby to hold at bedtime. This could also be done for separations. Suggest that there be a quiet time just before the child goes to bed, so he can have a chance to calm down. Rough and tumble play (jumping on the bed) should be discouraged.

Good-bye routine Help the mother settle on a routine to help her child with separations. Ask, "How will you say goodbye?" Make suggestions, like one hug, one kiss. The toddler could give the parent a push out the door. Routines will vary with the age of the child.

DEVELOPMENTAL INFORMATION

Separation is a major issue during the first three years of life. Babies need to feel secure in the constancy of their world and experiences. Then they can predict that parents return and their needs will be met. They create mental images of the experiences that they can recall in times of discomfort which helps them develop self-regulation and later impulse control. At various times during the first three years, babies will be more resistant to separations. They will cry and cling to parents. These are signs of a meaningful relationship and a baby's growing awareness of cognitive/learning categories (e.g., familiar and unfamiliar people.) Going to sleep is another kind of separation that can be difficult for some children. When young children go to sleep they are not sure the objects in their environment will continue to exist and will still be there when they wake up. For these children, out of sight is truly out of mind. Establishing a nighttime routine helps a baby to relax and enjoy going to bed. Having a routine and feeling secure about the constancy of care will help babies learn ways to calm themselves when upset. This self-regulation is the forerunner of impulse control and socialization.

3

Reunion routine   Establish a meaningful greeting like a name, hug, or verbalization, when reuniting after a brief separation.

Memory book   Take pictures of the baby with his mother. Let her write her perspective on what the photo shows and what her baby's perspective might be.

Literacy Connection   Label objects for the baby. Walk around the room with the baby, pointing and labeling objects similar to those found in the story book.

Parent-child issues   Parents sometimes resist their babies' clinging, especially when they become toddlers. Bedtime struggles can also be an issue. Parents should not be afraid to set firm limits. Limits can be set in peaceful ways, especially once parents have established a routine and offer to engage in a quiet activity with the child.

Encourage the mother to put her child to bed when she does not feel so tired and stressed that she is likely to lose patience quickly.

Me and My Body

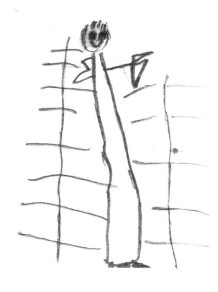

GOAL	The child will develop a sense of body self and self-regulation.
AGE	Birth to 36 months
PURPOSE	To help babies learn to identify parts of the body. This activity should be fun and should not emphasize learning for learning's sake. Parents can show approval of the baby's body and help the baby discover a sense of the physical body.

ACTIVITY   Before one year of age and during routine times such as diapering and feeding, the mother can conversationally name parts of the body. For example she might say while diapering, "Oh, there's your leg," as she touches his leg, and, "I have to move your leg out of the way," as she moves his leg. Encourage her to say whatever is appropriate in the situation. This activity can be done during bathing and other routines. As the baby grows older the mother can make a game of this activity, first by touching the baby's body, (e.g., his nose), and saying, "There's baby's nose." She can then take the baby's hand and touch her own nose, saying, "There's mommy's nose." She can repeat this for facial features such as the nose, mouth, eyes, and ears. Later she can add cheeks, eyelids, and eyebrows. During the second year, the mother can add the whole face. She can say something like, "There are your eyes, and there is your nose. Those are all parts of your face."

MORE ACTIVITIES   This activity can also be done while standing in front of the mirror (See **"Mirror, Mirror"** p. 9) The mother can also do baby exercises and talk about the motion of the baby's body part. For example, the mother can say, "I'm swinging your leg (or arm) up," with the emphasis on the positional word, "up", "down", "in", "out".

While dressing the baby, she can label the parts of the body, perhaps by singing the following rhyme (tune: "The Farmer in the Dell"):

> The socks go on the feet
> The socks go on the feet
> We are having lots of fun
> The socks go on the feet.

This can be repeated while dressing the baby in other items of clothing (e.g., shirt goes over the head, etc.).

ENDING THE ACTIVITY   Every activity should have a verbal warning that it is ending. The mother could say something like, "One more time up and we'll stop." Tell the child what they are going to do next. The mother could say, "Now, we'll get ready to go outside, ...to the store...take a bath...eat your lunch...play on the floor...take a nap." The mother should select the description that is most appropriate for the next activity.

DEVELOPMENTAL INFORMATION

Young children have to learn a sense of an integrated body and the relationship of one part to another. They learn where their body is in relation to others (where self ends and another self begins). This learning is necessary in order for children to develop self-control. This activity will provide babies with a sense of boundaries and will help them develop a positive attitude toward themselves physically.

DEVELOPMENTAL TEACHING

Share the above information with the mother. Make this activity fun, and don't insist that the baby name or point to every part on his body. Starting in the first year, the mother can begin this activity while diapering and feeding the baby.

5

Stop and Go

GOAL   The child will develop a sense of body self and self-regulation.

AGE   3 to 18 months

PURPOSE   To help develop self-concept as the child learns about inner and outer experiences and develops the capacity for self-regulation.

ACTIVITY   The father can play some music or sing a song for his baby. When the music starts, he holds his baby and dances or moves around the room, making sure the baby gets the feel of movement. The father stops the music and stops the dance. Repeat this several times.

MORE ACTIVITIES   As the baby gets older the father can bounce his baby on his knee or hip or swing the baby by holding her facing outward. As she is able to stand and then walk, the father can hold hands and dance and stop to the music. When the baby can walk independently, she can be encouraged to dance and stop on her own. This activity can also be performed with the father sitting in a rocking chair or a swing while holding the baby.

The father should vary the type of music that is played and dance accordingly. Soft music should be used with slower dance steps for infants, adding more rousing music as the baby gets older. Even for older babies, soft music should be played from time to time. When the baby becomes an independent walker, the father can put on softer music and let his toddler continue to dance.

As the baby gets older, the father can use music as a signal for ending activities. When the music stops, the father can say to the baby, "The dance is over. We had such fun dancing. We danced and stopped." He can also clap his and his baby's hands with the music, and stop clapping when the music ends. Use familiar melodies for this activity. Instead of using music, the parent can chant. For instance, "We walk and we walk and we walk and we stop." Pause before repeating the chant. Other examples include, "We clap," "We wiggle," "We jump," etc.

ENDING THE ACTIVITY   The father can use the final part of music as a signal for another activity to begin. "When the song is over, it will be time to turn out the light and go to sleep."

DEVELOPMENTAL INFORMATION

To help develop self-concept as the child learns about inner and outer experiences and develops the capacity for self-regulation

---

DEVELOPMENTAL TEACHING

Help the parent understand how important it is for babies to develop a sense of regularity in areas like coming and going, starting and stopping. Self-regulation helps a child to gain self-control. At about three years of age, when a sense of self is firmly established, the child has a greater capacity for self-control and compliance with parental requests.

Mirror, Mirror

GOAL   The child will develop a sense of body self and self-regulation.

AGE   8 to 18 months

PURPOSE   To have parents help the baby develop knowledge of parts of the body. This activity also gives the opportunity to introduce names and labels for various parts of the body.

ACTIVITY   This activity is most appropriate for bathing, diapering, dressing, or feeding times. Encourage the mother to hold her baby in front of a mirror, point to various parts of his body, and label them. "This is baby's eye, this is baby's ear," and so on. When the baby is about one year old, the mother can reverse the game and ask her baby, "Where is baby's nose?" or, "Where is mommy's nose?" The mother can also point to her own eyes, nose, and label these parts.

MORE ACTIVITIES   During baby's bath, encourage the mother to talk about parts of the baby's body as she washes them. Touching, along with the name, will help the baby develop a mental image of his body. This image will foster self-concept and a sense of body boundaries. The mother can also name other items associated with the bath. They can talk about sensations of warm water, rough or smooth cloth, cold air, soft arms or warm towels.

The mother can make this activity interactive by pointing to the baby's nose, then asking him to point to his own nose. Vary the game by asking baby to point to mommy's nose while the mother points to the baby's nose. Continue with eyes, ears, mouth, and hair. Add chin, cheeks, and neck as baby gets older.

Say this rhyme: **Heads, Shoulders, Knees and Toes**
Heads, shoulders, knees and toes, knees and toes
Heads, shoulders, knees and toes, knees and toes
And eyes and ears and mouth and nose
Head, shoulders, knees and toes, knees and toes

Or say this rhyme: A butterfly came to visit me
First it landed on my knee
Then it tried to taste my toes
And now it's sitting on my nose

Or sing this rhyme to the tune of **The Farmer in the Dell**:
These are your feet
These are your feet
Hi ho the Derry-oh
These are your feet

Repeat the rhyme with other parts of the body: hands, fingers, arms, legs, toes, etc.

DEVELOPMENTAL INFORMATION

After about six months of age, one task for the baby is to learn that he is separate from other individuals. This is the beginning of the development of a concept of self. Holding, cuddling, and patting the baby are some of the ways that help him learn about his physical boundaries. Identifying the parts of the body helps the baby learn about his body, how it works, and how he can control parts of it.

DEVELOPMENTAL TEACHING

Share the above information with the mother. Help her find ways to help her baby see how he is different from other people. The mother can use words like "you" and "me", or refer to the baby by his name and the adult by her name or title. For instance, she could say, "Mommy is giving (baby's name) a bath." This activity can also help the mother become more observant of her baby, and know him better.

ENDING THE ACTIVITY   Continue this type of activity as the baby is being dressed, naming the part of the body as clothes are put on or over him. Comment on some behavioral attribute of the baby in a positive way, saying, "You helped mommy by holding up your arm; what a good helper." Hold, hug or pat the part of the baby's body that is involved (e.g., patting the baby's arm after putting his shirt on, the leg after putting the pants on). Make a statement about what will happen next.

SUGGESTED BOOKS

Where is Baby's Belly Button?	Karen Katz Little (Simon, 2000)
Babies	Lara Holtz (Darling Kindersley, 2002)

Fingers and Toes

GOAL The child will develop a sense of body self and self-regulation.

AGE Birth to 18 months

PURPOSE To help children and parents discover the child as a source of enjoyment. This is an appropriate activity for initiating a discussion about anything to do with a child's developing sense of physical self, control, and appropriate handling of the child's body.

ACTIVITY Have the mother describe her childhood memories of these interactional games. Talk about the activity as well as the feelings generated. Most of these games involve touching and counting fingers or toes while engaging in a conversation with the baby.

This Little Piggy
This little piggy went to market; this little piggy stayed home;
This little piggy had roast beef and this little piggy had none;
(During these two lines the parent touches the toes in turn, starting with the big toe to the fourth toe.)
And this little piggy went, wee, wee, wee, all the way home.
(This is said while the parent touches little toe, then creeps fingers up to baby's shoulder.)

MORE ACTIVITIES The mother can modify the activity incorporating those activities her baby would be familiar with, "This little piggy's in the bathtub; this little piggy is not." Encourage the mother to use games that she experienced when she was young, or which are part of her culture. Simple hand clapping games might be useful here such as:

Miss Mary Mack
Miss Mary Mack, Mack, Mack
All dressed in black, black, black
With silver buttons, buttons, buttons
All down her back, back, back

She asked her mother, mother, mother
For fifteen cents, cents, cents
To see the elephants, elephants, elephants
Jump the fence, fence, fence

They jumped so high, high, high
They touched the sky, sky, sky
And they didn't get back, back, back
'Til the Fourth of July, ly, ly.

Hold the baby and move to the directions of songs like the **Hokey Pokey** and **Head, Shoulders, Knees, and Toes.**

ENDING THE ACTIVITY Every activity should have a verbal warning that it is ending. Say something like, "One more time." Tell the baby what will happen next.

DEVELOPMENTAL INFORMATION

A major task for infants is to learn the difference between self and others. Babies store this information in the brain as an image of self and an image of others caring for them. This will eventually allow the baby to keep the sense of self even when upset or feeling bad. Babies learn these differences between self and others by coming into close physical contact with adults. Babies really learn where their bodies end and another begins by touching or being touched by others. Physical body games are an appropriate and enjoyable way to engage in close physical contact and touch.

DEVELOPMENTAL TEACHING

Share the above information with the mother. Talk about the physical characteristics of her baby. Encourage the mother to share her view of her baby. Talk about the baby's appearance or physical development. Focus on the pleasure the mother gets when holding her baby close. This activity also gives an opportunity to explore the mother's childhood, and discuss what type of body games her parents played with her. There are also cultural variations of some of these games like **"This Little Piggy,"** and the mother can play her family versions with her baby.

11

DEVELOPMENTAL INFORMATION

During the first few months of life, babies are just learning about the important people in their lives. How caregivers respond to the infant's needs will guide the development of future relationships, self-concept, and self-esteem. If the infant receives signals that he is worthy of nurturing care, the baby will develop a positive feeling of regard for self. At the same time, developing communication with adult partners will aid in language development and assist with separations from significant persons later on in development. This activity focuses the parent's attention on the baby and allows both of them to enjoy their time together. It also draws the baby's attention to the person who is causing him to feel good. In this way, attachment to that person is promoted.

DEVELOPMENTAL TEACHING

Share the above information with the father. Ask him to think about those persons with whom he has a close relationship. Discuss the reasons for those feelings. Focus on things that might show how his own needs are being met. Relate this information to the baby's needs, and how good feelings emerge when needs are met. Explain how taking turns plays a role in language development. Use your interactions with the father to illustrate how language has played a part in developing his relationship with the Home Visitor. Finally, encourage the father to have fun and show enjoyment in his interaction with his baby.

GOAL The child will develop an understanding of how things work and how to make things happen.

AGE Birth to 8 months

PURPOSE To foster a relationship that will help the child in developing a self-concept and a sense of self in relation to the primary caregiver. Taking turns is also important in developing early social language.

ACTIVITY The father should hold his baby about eight to twelve inches away so that they can make eye contact. **In this activity the parent takes the first turn** by making a positive statement to his baby, (e.g., "What a nice baby you are.") This exchange should be continued in order to engage his baby's interest and attention. Comments can be made playfully, and in a slightly higher pitched voice. When the baby is watching closely, the father should stop talking, keep the baby in position and wait for him to respond. When the baby responds, the father should smile, and maintain eye contact. When the baby stops vocalizing, the father takes another turn. Repeat these steps several times so that both father and child take a few turns.

MORE ACTIVITIES Discuss with the father how this language activity might change as the baby grows older. For example, the father can turn the activity into a game of "Show Me," by asking the baby to point to body parts or pictures in a book.

Emphasize the importance of the father's exaggerating his inflections so his baby learns about variations in tone.

ENDING THE ACTIVITY Observe when the baby might be tiring of the game. End the activity by saying something like, "It looks like you're finished playing this game, but I had a good time talking with you (being with you). We'll do it again, soon." The father could also say "I love you," or, "I love being with you," and then hug or pat the baby. Remind the father that even though his baby doesn't talk yet, he will pick up the feeling of the father's enjoyment through the tone of his voice. The father can end the activity by telling his baby what they are going to do next.

What I want to bring out is how a pebble cast into a pond causes ripples that spread in all directions. And each one of our thoughts, words and deeds is like that.

- Dorothy Day

13

Please Mother, I Want to do it Myself

GOAL The child will develop an understanding of how things work and how to make things happen.

AGE 6 to 18 months

PURPOSE To help children be participants in care routines.

ACTIVITY At mealtime encourage the mother to cut up small pieces of food (the size of a raisin) so the baby can finger feed. It's natural for babies to put everything in their mouths.

MORE ACTIVITIES As the child gets older give the child her own spoon so she may "help" feed herself. When the baby tries to dip the spoon into the food, the mother can help by placing the food on the spoon and directing the food to her baby's mouth. This does not have to be done for the entire meal. A few self-feeding attempts will usually satisfy the child.

At bath time the mother can give her baby her own washcloth to use while the mother bathes her. The mother can provide an empty shampoo bottle or measuring cup for baby to use to fill and rinse.

The mother can sing or chant songs like:

Rub a Dub Dub, Three Men In a Tub
Rub a dub dub, three men in a tub,
And who do you think they be?
The butcher, the baker, the candlestick maker,
And they all went to sea.

Rain Rain
Rain, rain, go away, come again another day.
Little (child's name) wants to play.

ENDING THE ACTIVITY Describe what the baby is doing. Use "Baby's Story," on page 47 as a guide. End the activity by saying something like, "There, the bath is over, and you helped Mommy by washing your leg." Then describe what is going to happen next, or what you are doing for baby, saying for example, "Now, I'll wipe your hands and put you on the floor to play while I clean up."

DEVELOPMENTAL INFORMATION

At the height of the attachment to her mother, at about four or five months of age, the baby begins to work on becoming a separate and independent being, a person in her own right. Early evidence of this development is the baby's attempt to imitate others and participate in her own care. Increasing independence should go along with increasing competence and should help foster separation and a sense of self.

DEVELOPMENTAL TEACHING

Explain that sometimes babies want to feed themselves. As the baby develops fine motor skills, the mother can allow her baby to participate more fully in feeding time. Help the mother understand that this trying to feed herself is not a deliberate effort to interfere with care. It is the baby's natural tendency to imitate the parent and to begin to show signs of independence and self-care. **Responsibility for oneself is a desirable attribute and has its root in this first year of life.**

Lunch Time

GOAL The child will develop an understanding of how things work and how to make things happen.

AGE 10 to 36 months

PURPOSE This activity deals with the developmental issue of dropping objects, watching them fall and wanting them to be retrieved. This is sometimes difficult for parents who may become tired of cleaning up food or playing the retrieving objects game.

SITUATION Mrs. Williams put 12 month old Shawna in her high chair for lunch. Knowing that Shawna could feed herself, the mother gave her an assortment of finger foods to munch while she fed the baby. Bit by bit Shawna dropped the food on the floor. When it was all gone, Shawna began to cry. Mrs. Williams put the baby down just long enough to give Shawna some Cheerios. A minute later the cereal was on the floor and Shawna started to cry again.

WHAT TO TELL THE PARENT The mother acted appropriately in responding to Shawna's distress. She didn't punish Shawna for playing with her food or for crying. Help the mother decide how she might be available for Shawna's feeding. She might sit close enough to Shawna so that she can offer her food occasionally during the meal. She might also give Shawna some toys to play with that would be all right for her to toss over the side of the high chair (e.g., a small rubber ball, rattles, or small stuffed toys). Remind the mother to make clean-up or retrieval easier by placing a cloth or newspaper under the high chair.

When the mother sits nearby, she can talk to Shawna about how she is eating and how the baby is eating. Shawna will know that she is being noticed by her mother and is being included in the larger social unit with the baby.

MORE ACTIVITIES The mother could give Shawna a small dish of Cheerios and let her sit with her on the couch as she feeds the baby. Remind Shawna that she will have special time with Mom when the baby takes his nap.

At this stage, it might be appropriate to offer a small fork to Shawna at mealtime. This novelty could help Shawna focus her attention on eating, making eating more interesting, foster her motor skills, and develop her independence.

ENDING THE ACTIVITY Remind the mother to continue to show attention to Shawna, and include her in the baby's daily care routines. She could say, "What a wonderful help you are. (Baby's name) is lucky to have you for a big sister."

DEVELOPMENTAL INFORMATION

At this age, a child learns about the nature of objects. An object falling looks different from that same object lying on a high chair tray. Dropping objects is not unusual behavior for a child of this age. However, in Shawna's situation, there may be other factors contributing to her behavior. This behavior may be her way of showing that she still wants her mother's presence and help while eating. This type of game gives children some control over adult behavior at a time when they are getting ready to make a move towards independence.

Shake, Rattle and Roll

I look in the mirror through the eyes of the child that was me.

- Judy Collins

GOAL The child will develop an understanding of how things work and how to make things happen.

AGE 6 to 12 months

PURPOSE To help children develop a sense of accomplishment, and to integrate sensory information, by associating objects with their sound.

ACTIVITY For this activity, use plastic eggs such as those in which pantyhose are purchased or those that are sold in discount stores. Empty film cans also work well, and they are very hard to open.

Fill the egg with some small objects such as dried lima beans, a small wooden spool, small bells, or macaroni. Secure the egg so it cannot be opened. Strapping tape or electrical tape, one inch wide, can be used. Give the egg to the baby to shake or roll on the floor. Talk with the baby about what is being done with the egg, and the result. For example, the father can say, "You are shaking that egg so hard. Listen to the loud noise you are making." "You are barely moving the egg and it's making such a soft sound." When the baby stops shaking the container, make a statement about the noise stopping.

MORE ACTIVITIES Make several eggs with different objects inside. The father can then talk about the differences in sounds among the different eggs, and how the baby can change the intensity of the sound. Again, make sure the eggs are well secured and cannot come apart. An adult should always supervise this activity.

ENDING THE ACTIVITY Every activity should have a verbal warning that it is ending. The baby will probably end this game on his own. However, if it must be ended before the baby tires of it, say something like, "One more time and we'll put the toys away." Again, tell him what is going to happen next.

DEVELOPMENTAL INFORMATION

Babies learn about the world through their senses. At approximately six months of age, babies have sufficient control to grasp and shake objects. They can control the sound and begin to learn the relationship between action (shaking and the intensity of shaking) and outcome (intensity of sound). This activity allows babies to manipulate objects and control the sights and sounds objects make.

DEVELOPMENTAL TEACHING

Share the above information with the father. Help him make this toy and use it to interact with his baby.

A Rose by Any Other Name

Snowflakes, leaves, humans, plants, raindrops, stars, molecules, microscopic entities all come in communities.
The singular cannot in reality exist.
- Paula Gunn Allen

DEVELOPMENTAL INFORMATION

Names are often tied to self-concept and identity. Parents sometimes name a baby after a family member, friend, or hero. In other instances parents might make up a name for the baby. Names are sometimes based on a fantasy the parents have about the baby. This activity provides an opportunity to talk about self-concept as it is reflected through the parent's eyes, and as it is evoked in the baby, based on perceptions of the name and other people's reactions to the name (e.g., "That's an interesting name," or, "That's a pretty name.")

DEVELOPMENTAL TEACHING

Talk about ways that names might influence perceptions of the baby and interactions with her. Emphasize the importance of calling the baby by her name. Sometimes parents have nicknames for their baby. This would be a good time to talk about the appropriateness of those names, and the appropriate time to use the baby's real name. In families with twins the discussion might focus on helping the babies develop separate identities, especially if the names are similar in pronunciation, as with John and Shawn.

GOAL The baby will develop trust through secure attachments and meaningful relationships.

AGE Birth to 12 months

PURPOSE To get the mother talking about a positive aspect of her relationship with her baby. This activity might also elicit warm or humorous family stories and focus the mother on what she enjoys about her baby.

ACTIVITY During a home visit start a discussion about names. Start with mother's name or the baby's name. Make a positive or neutral comment about the name if possible (e.g., "I like that name.") Focus on the baby's name and how it was chosen.. You might extend this to family names, in general. Ask the mother to tell stories about her family and how family members were named.

MORE ACTIVITIES If the mother seems interested in this discussion you could ask if she likes her name, or if she is satisfied with the baby's name. Then ask the mother what name she would have chosen for herself if she had been given a choice.

Start a discussion about the origin of the names of grandparents, aunts, uncles, and cousins. Demonstrate how names connect to each family member's particular personality and history.

Discuss the appropriateness of the baby's name with her personality. Discuss ways the baby's name might influence how the mother views the baby, especially if she was named for a relative or friend.

Discuss ways that names are meaningful and influence the self-image and identity of each person. Talk about whether or not names influence personality and social interactions. All of these discussions should focus on promoting positive relationships within the family, and between the mother and her baby.

ENDING THE ACTIVITY When it is time to move on, make a closing comment. If the mother has been positive about the baby and her name, say something like, "It's good to hear you talk so warmly about your baby." If the comments were negative, say something about babies changing as they grow and develop. Talk about how parents play a very big role in that growth. The intent of this discussion is not to moralize or dismiss the mother's feelings, but to support her in her current situation while projecting optimism for the future. Ask the mother directly for positive comments about the baby or the baby's best feature or most endearing quality. Discuss how the mother can influence her baby's future behavior and provide some suggestions.

Conversations - Before You Came

*It isn't enough
to talk about peace.
One must believe in it.
And it isn't
enough to believe in it.
One must work at it.*
— Eleanor Roosevelt

GOAL The baby will develop trust through secure attachments and meaningful relationships.

AGE Birth to 12+ months

PURPOSE To help the mother talk about a positive aspect of her relationship with her baby.

ACTIVITY During the home visit, find a time when the mother seems positively disposed toward her baby. Suggest that she hold the child, cradled in her arms. Have the mother look into her baby's eyes and talk to him. The conversation should focus around the mother's experiences during pregnancy and what she would like the baby to know. She can share her aspirations, hopes, dreams and goals, and relate how the baby was named. If the mother finds this difficult, or starts to give negative accounts, accept that, at least initially. Probe gently, saying for example, "Did you think about what kind of baby (or adult) he would be?" If the mother still doesn't give any information, move on to something else.

MORE ACTIVITIES Have the mother keep a journal that can be written in letter form. She can dictate the content to the Home Visitor who then returns it to be placed in the family's memory book.

The mother can write a letter to be opened by the child at a later age, or on his third birthday, or whenever the child shows an interest in mail.

ENDING THE ACTIVITY Encourage the mother to continue to talk to her baby about his accomplishments and how proud she is of his many attributes.

DEVELOPMENTAL INFORMATION

Tell the mother that a child is often interested in the time she was waiting for her baby to be born and is also curious about what he was like as a newborn Sometimes mothers are hesitant to talk about his family history and background. If, however, mothers begin to talk about the baby as an emerging "person," they can also begin to imagine the baby's future. At the same time, the mother's hopes and dreams for her child become more realistic. Conversations about the waiting period can help the mother talk about her feelings and experiences which then will promote stronger bonds between the mother and her baby.

DEVELOPMENTAL TEACHING

Children learn about babies out of their own curiosity. For example, they see babies in their neighborhood, with relatives, at daycare, in books, etc. As they become aware that babies grow inside their mothers, they will often ask questions about their own mothers' experience. Such questions give the mother a chance to talk with her child about waiting for her baby and his arrival.

Praise Phrases

Yet even more important than role modeling is love…
- M. Scott Peck

GOAL The baby will develop trust through secure attachments and meaningful relationships.

AGE Birth to 36 months

PURPOSE To help children develop a positive self-concept and positive self-esteem.

ACTIVITY During the home visit, talk with the mother about what accomplishments her baby has acquired over the past few weeks. Suggest that she practice different phrases that can be said to support and reinforce the learning. Develop a list of five to ten phrases and practice how to say them to the child. Write down different scenarios to leave with the mother. For example, when the baby learns to smile, the mother could say any of the following: "Oh, what a nice smile." "That smile lights up the room." "That smile makes my day." "I feel really good when you smile at me." The mother should smile back at her while adding something like, "That smile shows me you're happy," or "I think you must like what I'm doing with you. You're smiling." Encourage the mother to give hugs or pats during the praise. Physical contact adds to the pleasure of both parent and child.

MORE ACTIVITIES Have the mother identify two or three new things her baby has learned during the week. Write them down, or have her write them down along with the praise phrase. Keep them in a scrap book with the baby's age and the date.

When the baby learns a new skill such as turning over, creeping or crawling, take her picture and label it with the date and her age. Develop appropriate praise phrases for each photo.

ENDING THE ACTIVITY Ask the mother to end this activity with a positive general statement about everything the baby has been learning or doing that pleases her. She can say, "You're smiling and cooing," and "It's so nice to see you learning all of these things." Tell the baby what will happen next.

SUGGESTED BOOKS

Peekaboo Morning   Rachel Isadora (Putnam's Sons, 2002)

I Kissed the Baby   Mary Murphy (Candlewick Press, 2004)

DEVELOPMENTAL INFORMATION

From birth, babies need to have a sense that they are worthwhile and pleasing to their parents. That sense of worth is most easily gained through regular and consistent caregiving that meets the baby's needs. However, helping parents notice and comment on their baby's accomplishments, especially in giving praise, will also help the babies feel good about themselves. When babies feel good and connect that feeling to a parent or caregiver, they are more likely to make positive and meaningful connections with that person. Later, during the second year of life, when adults set limits for the children, they will be more likely to respond positively.

DEVELOPMENTAL TEACHING

Share the above information with the mother. Ask her to observe the baby or child during certain activities or routines. This can be done before the home visit.

25

Journals - How You've Grown

*With every deed you
are sowing a seed,
though the harvest
you may never see.*
- Ella Wheeler Wilcox

GOAL   The child will develop trust through secure attachments and meaningful relationships.

AGE   Birth to 36 months

PURPOSE   To focus parent's attention on how the baby has grown and changed over time.

ACTIVITY   Help the mother make a scrapbook, or buy an inexpensive notebook. Encourage her to make weekly entries detailing what the baby has learned, or what she has been working on learning during the last few days or over the course of a week. Help her write these in the journal with her baby's age and the date. Reinforce the mother's relationship with her baby and ways she is helping her grow and learn.

MORE ACTIVITIES   The mother can use phrases like "You used to be… or do…. Now you can…." to focus on how her baby is changing and growing. Add photographs to the weekly entries.

ENDING THE ACTIVITY   Encourage the mother to talk with the baby about what is going on and what will happen next. Tell her that you will look at the journal again.

DEVELOPMENTAL INFORMATION

A baby's growth is rapid during the first years of life. Sometimes parents may miss some of the subtleties of development, such as her attempts to roll over. Sensitive babies will sometimes think that no one is there to help or encourage their new skills. They may stop trying to do something, or may not try as hard. They may start to rely on themselves for the help they need. Toddlers may go and get the cookie they want instead of asking or relying on the adult to read their cues. They may also go beyond their limits, entering into harmful situations.

DEVELOPMENTAL TEACHING

Share the above information with the mother. Help her focus on stages of development by identifying characteristics associated with a particular stage. Give her strategies for helping her baby. A baby trying to roll over can be helped by positioning her arms and legs, and by providing toys just out of her reach as incentives. Tell the mother that placing her baby on a blanket on the floor with toys just out of her reach also encourages creeping and crawling.

Conversations - When You Were a Baby

World peace starts right here. I will not raise my child to kill your child.

— Barbara Choo

GOAL   The baby will develop trust through secure attachments and meaningful relationships.

AGE   Birth to 8 months

PURPOSE   To encourage parents to talk about the baby's attributes and pleasing qualities. Conversations also help the parent focus on positive interactions with the baby. Varied ways of communicating with a baby might include talking, writing, or singing.

ACTIVITY   Find a time when the mother is holding the baby, cradled in her arms. Have her look into the baby's eyes and talk to him. The conversation should focus around the baby's development during the first six to eight months of life. Help the mother identify the milestones her baby has achieved. By modeling, help her name these for the baby (e.g., "When you were just two months old you began to smile at me. That was an exciting time for me.") She could also describe bath times, his food preferences, his reactions to siblings, or vice versa. She should focus on things she would like the baby to know and things she would like to share with him about herself. Encourage her to share her feelings and reactions about her baby. She might discuss changes in perceptions, feelings, or hopes. She might talk about unpleasant things like changing diapers and getting up at night.

If the mother starts to say negative things to the baby about him or his impact on her, gently change the subject. However, it is important to make a note of what she said so it can be discussed with a supervisor at a later meeting.

MORE ACTIVITIES   Have the mother keep a journal that could be in letter form. She can dictate her comments which will be returned to her for her memory book. Suggest that she take a picture of her baby every month or so. Help her paste this in her journal or scrapbook along with the writing. These items can also be stored in a memory box.

ENDING THE ACTIVITY   Help the mother end on a positive note with regard to her baby. Encourage her to give him a comforting touch, pat or hug.

DEVELOPMENTAL INFORMATION

There are several important milestones in the first six to eight months of life that parents should note. Baby's first smile is something that often causes joy within families. Many families may not be aware that the baby has a preference for the mother (the primary caregiver) and will smile at her more often. She can elicit a smile when others cannot, indicating that her baby recognizes her from all other adults who might also care for the baby. Babies also begin to make sounds and imitate the sounds of others. They have differentiated cries for pain, for hunger, and even when they just want to be close or held by their mothers.

All of these developmental capacities gives babies the ability to connect with others, especially those important persons who provide the nurturing, care, and security that builds trust and close relationships.

DEVELOPMENTAL TEACHING

Share the above information with the mother. Discuss some of the ways she notices her baby responding to her care. Ask her to talk about her baby's responses that make her feel good as a mother and some that frustrate her.

Memory Book

We are tomorrow's past.
- May Webb

GOAL The child will develop trust through secure attachments and meaningful relationships.

AGE Birth to 36 months

PURPOSE To help parents and children mark special events in their lives, focusing on relationships as well as events around them. This activity is particularly good when children are changing caregivers, moving from one place to another, or in some other way experiencing changes in their lives, including growing up and learning new skills. It helps the young child deal with separations and changes by providing a memory aid.

ACTIVITY Work with the mother to make a memory book. For the cover punch holes in construction paper, poster board or pieces of cardboard cut roughly in paper size (8.5 x 11 inches). More construction paper can be used for the inside pages. The child can decorate the cover and the mother can write her child's name and Memory Book on the cover. On inside pages different events can be listed, such as moving, first day care experience, first time at church, etc. Periodically the Home Visitor can take pictures of the child or have the mother take pictures, if she has a camera. The pictures can highlight the child in his current house or bedroom, playing with toys, in child care, or relating to staff. These can then be pasted in the book or stored in a box.

MORE ACTIVITIES The child can draw pictures of his experiences on some of the pages and the mother can label the photos and drawings for her. An older child could provide his own labels and comments about the photos and art work. He might be able to dictate stories about the experiences for his mother to write in the book. If the event involves a physical move and change of residence, add pictures of the new location. The child might also want to take small mementos, such as a few pretty stones from his yard or grounds. Add information about the child at the time: his height, weight, favorite foods, for example.

Read the Memory Book to the child from time to time. Even babies will benefit from hearing about these special events.

Create a book about "Moving Day" if the family moves. Use simple stick figures to symbolize the process in pictures. This allows for individualization of the story about moving so that family members can draw or write about significant details.

Label the book "My Home," and include photos or drawings of the exterior of the house, street signs, and other interesting sights on the street. If possible, include photos of different rooms in the house.

ENDING THE ACTIVITY End the activity by assuring the child of the stability of the current living arrangement, the day care setting, or regarding the hopes for the family. Say something about enjoying the activity and tell the child what is going to happen next.

DEVELOPMENTAL INFORMATION

During the first three years children are working on establishing a solid sense of self. This development occurs in relationship to meaningful adults, most notably the parents. As children grow and behave they are sensitive to the reaction of parents as affirmation of their abilities and "goodness". They are also dependent on the parents for care and nurture. Until they have a sense of competence, children tend to resist separation from their parents and are stressed when they are away from them for long periods of time.

One of the reasons that separation is difficult at this age is that a child's memory is not fully developed. Younger children, under 18-20 months, have difficulty keeping an image of a parent in mind and calling up that image in times of stress. Older children can use this memory as reassurance of their parents' continued availability even when they are not around. When children move from place to place too frequently, or when they move to a new group or a new house, the mental adjustments needed to recreate their world in their mind can cause stress. Children can be relieved of some of this stress by having pictures or mementos of their previous situation.

CONTINUED

SUGGESTED BOOKS

Daddy and I	Eloise Greenfield (Writers and Readers, 1981)
Say Goodnight	Helen Oxenbury (Simon & Schuester, 1991)
Good Night, Baby	Clara Vulliamy (Candlewick Press, 1996)
Good Night Lily	Martha Alexander (Candlewick Press, 1993)
On My Own	Miela Ford (Greenwillow, 1999)
Mama, Mama	Jean Marzollo (Harper Collins Child Books, 1999)
Goodnight Moon	Margaret Wise Brown (Harper Collins Child Books, 1977)
Bye-Bye, Babies!	Angela Shelf Medearis (Candlewick Press, 1995)
Maybe My Baby	Irene O'Book (Harper Collins Child Books, 1998)
Me Too	Susan Winter (DK Publications, Inc., 1993)
On the Day I was Born	Debbi Chocolate (Scholastic, Inc., 1995)
ABC, I Like Me	Nancy Carlson (Puffin Books, 1999)

Memories of our lives, of our works and our deeds will continue in others.
- Rosa Parks

Leaving

GOAL   The child will develop trust through secure attachments and meaningful relationships.

AGE   6 to 12 months

DEVELOPMENTAL INFORMATION

Toward the end of the first year babies develop the ability to remember familiar persons. Troy, at seven months, has now learned that his mother is special and different from all other persons who care for him. He also has a dim awareness that she can leave. He has not had enough experience to know convincingly that she will return. All he knows is that he feels uncomfortable without her, so he protests her leaving. The crying that begins when the mother gathers her things together also means that Troy has begun to anticipate events and the discomfort (anxiety) that follows.

DEVELOPMENTAL TEACHING

Encourage this mother not to quit her job (even if she could), and encourage her to consider the developmental information presented above. Review with her the characteristics of development for babies at this age. When babies protest their mother's leaving it means they have learned that mother is a special person, and that they associate good feelings with that person. Reassure her that this is a stage of development and that the behavior will probably lessen or disappear in a few weeks. It would also be important not to make any other major changes for the baby at this time.

SITUATION   Seven-month-old Troy has always been a pleasant baby. He laughs easily, and readily accepts his mother's leaving. His caregiver, who has watched him since birth, adores him and gives him her full attention during the day. Just recently, however, he has started to cry in the morning when his mother gathers her work things together, even before they leave the house. He starts to wail when he sees the caregiver, continuing to cry more intensely when his mother walks out the door. During this time, nothing his caregiver does eases his distress. The mother has noticed similar behavior when she goes out in the evening. She feels like she should quit her job and stay home.

WHAT THE PARENT CAN DO   Support Troy in having a transition object and familiar play toys around when she is not there.

If Troy is cared for outside the home, the mother should work with the caregiver to minimize changes at this time. It would also be helpful for the mother to spend a little more time with him in the evening

Even though Troy is only seven months old, the mother can talk to him about the changes as she is getting ready for work. She can add that she'll miss him and tell him what she does at her job. (We don't know how much of this information will be understandable to Troy. But the fact that she is doing something positive might make her feel more relaxed and that could be transmitted to the baby.) She can add a constant phrase about always coming back saying, "Mommy will always come back to Troy."

If possible, the mother could stay a few minutes with the caregiver around, and come back to pick him up a few minutes early, so he is not the last child to leave. This is particularly important if care is provided outside the home.

Give the caregiver photographs of mother or of mother and Troy together. Post these on the walls on on Troy's crib or high chair.

Develop a ritual for saying good-bye, like walking to the window to wave to his mother as she leaves.

Let's Read

GOAL	The child will develop the ability to express feelings in appropriate ways.
AGE	Birth to 36 months
PURPOSE	To give children the opportunity to learn models for dealing with feelings and to provide opportunity to talk about feelings as they get older.

ACTIVITY   Story time can also be a sharing time. Encourage the father to tell stories about the day's activities, from his perspective, and then from his child's point of view. Include in the stories expression of feelings and motivation of characters. (She did this because....) Telling stories about conflicts will help his child get a better picture of how conflicts occur and are resolved. Keep in mind that these discussions should not be judgmental about good and bad, but should focus on problems and peaceful solutions.

Identify storybooks with related themes and read these to the child. This will let her know that she is not the only one to have certain feelings and concerns.

ENDING THE ACTIVITY   Always give the child time to talk about the story when it is over. Help her relate the story to her own experiences whenever appropriate. Talk about the pleasure both got from reading. Tell her what is going to happen next.

SUGGESTED BOOKS

Baby Faces	Margaret Miller (Simon & Schuster, 1998)
Happy Days	Margaret Miller (Simon & Schuster, 1996)
Smile!	Roberta Grobel Intrater (Scholastic, Inc., 1997)
My Many Colored Days	Dr. Seuss (Knopf, 1996)
Everywhere Babies	Susan Meyers (Harcourt , 2001)
On Monday When it Rained	Cherryl Kachenmeister (Houghton Mifflin, 1989)
When Sophie gets Angry	Molly Bang (Blue Sky Press, 1999)
No Biting!	Karen Katz (Grosset & Dunlap, 2002)

DEVELOPMENTAL INFORMATION
Reading stories to young children is one of the most important experiences they can have. Promoting relationships with adults requires time to sit and interact. Characters in books can be positive role models. Stories provide models of language structure and help children create their own stories. Reading stories promotes language development and vocabulary. **Children who are read to at home tend to become better readers.** Parents model ways of finding out information and share with children the joy of being competent readers and experiencing far away adventures, hopes and dreams. Even babies should be read to. At first it is the relationship that is most important, but as children grow they learn that reading is enjoyable. They can then experience for themselves the joy that hearing, then reading, stories can bring.

Big Friend, Little Friend   Eloise Greenfield (Writers & Readers, 1991)

I Kissed the Baby   Mary Murphy (Candlewick Press, 2003)

What Shall We Do With the Boo-Hoo Baby?   Cressida Cowell (Scholastic, 2001)

Counting Kisses   Karen Katz (McElderry/Simon & Schuster, 2002)

Nobody Asked Me if I Wanted a Baby Sister   Martha Alexander (Penguin Putnam Books, 1971)

If animals could vote, they would be against nuclear war.
- Mark M., Age 7

DEVELOPMENTAL TEACHING

Ask the father to recall some of the stories he heard when he was a child. Discuss his feelings about these experiences and the pleasure that being read to has provided. If he has not had good experiences with reading, or doesn't have confidence in his own reading ability, talk about that. Encourage him to identify oral stories he has heard that would be appropriate to share with his child. Help him identify and select appropriate books that he feels comfortable reading to his daughter. Encourage him to read daily and to make reading time pleasurable and interactive, rather than a rigid learning activity. Help the father have confidence that his child will learn a lot through reading activities, without being formally taught. Encourage him to pause while reading the story to allow her to reflect and respond to it as she grows and her language ability develops. He can encourage her to respond to pictures and anticipate the story line. For example, he could say, "Can you guess what will happen here?" Read stories over and over so the child can become familiar with them.

Let's Dance

GOAL	The child will develop the ability to express feelings in appropriate ways.
AGE	Birth to 36 months
PURPOSE	To give children the opportunity to move to music that reflects a variety of feelings such as calmness, anger, sadness, excitement and joy.

DEVELOPMENTAL INFORMATION

Physical activity is one of the baby's earliest means of expression. The scrunched up face indicates that a cry is coming even before it is heard. In the very early days, it might be the movement of hands and feet, not a smile, that lets us know that the baby is pleased. It is important to help the baby continue these physical ways of expressing feelings. Most parents do this naturally, holding the baby while rocking, stroking, and gliding with the infant in their arms.

ACTIVITY   As gets older, let him suggest the mood, music, and action. Encourage free movement to music of various kinds. The mother may want to dance with him, to increase the feeling of togetherness.

See the activity **"Stop and Go,"** p. 7 in an earlier section of this document.

Suggest that the mother share some of the movement games from her own childhood.

Two Little Hands
Two little hands go clap, clap, clap.
Two little feet go tap, tap tap.
One little leap up from the chair,
Two little arms go up in the air.
Two little hands go thump, thump, thump.
Two little feet go jump, jump, jump.
One little body goes round and round.
One little child sits quietly down.

ENDING THE ACTIVITY   Watch for signs of tiredness in the young baby and stop when he seems weary. Always tell the baby or child how enjoyable the activity was, and tell him what is going to happen next.

DEVELOPMENTAL TEACHING

Share the above information with the mother. Encourage her to talk about her feelings about dance, exercise, and other body movements or physical activity. Explore ways that she might feel comfortable moving with the baby. Explain that she can play music that is soft and slow for gliding around the room to calm her crying baby. As the baby gets older and starts to express feelings, the mother can use them as cues and put on music that reflects her baby's mood. Mother and baby then can move as the music suggests. Marches might be used for heavy stepping and lullabies for gentle rocking.

*Peace is knowing
that someone
cares about me.*
- Kim Minshall, 8th grade

Let's Sing

GOAL The child will develop the ability to express feelings in appropriate ways.

AGE Birth to 36 months

PURPOSE To help children express feelings and moods in various ways giving them the opportunity to hear a variety of language forms, such as songs, speech, or poetry.

ACTIVITY Help the mother identify times when her child can be sung to. Getting up and morning routines are great times for this to occur. The parent can take on an opera-like role, singing something like, "Oh, it's time to get up. I see you're awake, now. We'll go eat, now. I'll warm your bottle (fix your cereal), now." The mother can then resume regular talking interactions.

MORE ACTIVITIES There are some songs that are particularly suited to this activity. A good one is **"The Party's Over. It's time to call it a day."** The mother could sing this or make up words to the tune at the end of the day.

There are many children's songs that deal with routines such as sleeping, eating, getting up that can be used. Play and sing lullabies (**"Brahms Lullaby," "Hush Little Baby"**).

The mother can say something each night to cue her child that it's time to sleep. ("Good night. The moon is out. Tomorrow the sun will come up to say hello.")

Nursery rhymes or poems can be used and put to music and sung for the child.

Tapes of children's well-loved songs can be listened to while playing at home.

ENDING THE ACTIVITY Watch for signs that the baby is tired of this activity and needs some non-singing interaction and communication. Very young babies can be overwhelmed by volume or tempo of the singing. End with soft notes. Older children can tolerate more variety in tone, pitch and tempo. Comment on the transition to regular conversation. ("I just sang to you. Now I'm talking again. I like singing, and soon you'll be singing with me.") Always express delight with the interaction and reassure the child of your availability and love.

DEVELOPMENTAL INFORMATION

Music is an activity that is fun, easy, and beneficial to babies and young children. Music can be calming or exciting. Singing fosters language development. It gives a lighter tone when children have to be redirected or limited in activities. It's hard to be angry and still sing. Music can create an air of intimacy, an activity that has special meaning to two people in a relationship. Parents and children can have a special song or piece of music that has a definite meaning for just them.

DEVELOPMENTAL TEACHING

Share the above information with the mother. Ask her to recall music she liked when she was a child. Discuss whether the music was designed especially for children, or whether it was just popular music from that time. Talk about songs and music her child likes, and what its origin is. Many children know tunes from commercials and other television shows. Encourage mothers to broaden their exposure by playing a variety of music on the radio or other electronic devices.

Baby's Cry

To work in the world lovingly means that we are defining what we will be for, rather than reacting to what we are against.

— Christina Baldwin

GOAL The child will develop the ability to follow directions and accept limits.

AGE Birth to 36 months

PURPOSE To help parents understand the connection between crying as an expression of baby's needs and its place in the development of a positive relationship. To give parents strategies for coping with the stress they feel when babies cry for long periods or are difficult to comfort.

ACTIVITY Encourage the father to respond immediately to his baby's cry. Even if he doesn't physically pick up the baby, he can talk to her, letting her know the cry was heard. He can pat her back, use soothing words, or sing quiet songs.

If the father knows the cause (or can make a good guess) he should say that to the baby (e.g., "Oh, I know that cry. That means you're hungry".) That lets the baby know that her cry has been accepted as a communication. As babies grow in language they will tend to use words instead of acting out to get needs met.

Also, talk about the child's different types of crying. The sound of the cry may be different if the child is hurt, hungry, tired, fussy, angry, or in need of affection.

Hush! Be Still (Tune: Twinkle, Twinkle Little Star)
Hush! Be still as any mouse,
There's a baby in the house.
Not a dolly, not a toy,
But a laughing, crying boy (or girl).

DEVELOPMENTAL INFORMATION
Many adults think that picking up a crying baby too soon will spoil them and that these babies will become impulsive children who are non-compliant and difficult to manage. Just the opposite is true. When adults comfort crying babies in a minimal amount of time, they are likely to cry less, rather than more. Crying is the baby's way of communicating a need. If we don't respond quickly, we are telling the baby that the communication isn't working, or that we don't think the need is significant enough to be noticed by us. Since babies have no words to tell us what they want, they might start to disengage from the parent when the parent does not meet their needs.

MORE ACTIVITIES As babies get older, they are able to wait a little before needs are met so long as caregivers signal their readiness to meet the need. The father tells his baby he is getting the bottle or the diaper and can see if the baby stops crying. At six or seven months of age, babies associate the sound of a voice with the comforting behavior that follows, and will often stop crying at the sound of the voice alone. When that happens, the parent can make the connection verbally that the baby has made conditionally. Say something like, "You heard daddy's voice, and you knew that I would be bringing your bottle and you stopped crying."

When children get older you might encourage them to pretend their doll or stuffed animal is crying, and have them attend to the crying baby.

ENDING THE ACTIVITY Watch for signs of tiredness in the young baby and stop when she seems weary. Always tell the baby or child how enjoyable the activity was, and tell her what is going to happen next.

SUGGESTED BOOK

What Shall we do with the Boo-Hoo Baby?

Cressida Cowell (Scholastic, 2001)

*One day we must come to see that peace
is not merely a distant goal that we seek
but a means by which we arrive at that
goal. We must pursue peaceful
ends through peaceful means.*

\- Martin Luther King, Jr.

DEVELOPMENTAL TEACHING

Encourage the father to talk about his feelings associated with crying. Explore all of the reasons that crying might be annoying, including feelings of helplessness, especially when the baby is not easily comforted. Discuss the different messages the baby communicates by crying: hunger, pain, the need to be close or to be held, too much stimulation. Encourage the father to talk about the subtle changes in the cry that indicate one need or the other. Help him accept the cry as communication. Knowing baby's signals will lessen the father's uncertainty and decrease his uneasiness with crying.

This is a good opportunity to help the father cope with his reactions to a baby's cry. Rehearse methods to reduce his stress and look for signs that he may need extra help in learning to comfort his baby or manage his own feelings about a baby's distress.

Portraits

*The decisions
we make now affect
the seven generations
of children to come.*

- American Indian Wisdom

GOAL The child will develop the ability to follow directions and accept limits.

AGE Birth to 36 months

PURPOSE To let children have a glimpse of their own history. To sequence events in their lives and to talk about experiences that brought joy or sadness, happiness or anger.

ACTIVITY Encourage the mother to take photographs of her baby on some regular basis. If her resources are limited, help her determine what might be important events or ages to capture on film, and which might be recorded in written form only. Help her document the event in a scrapbook or journal, recording the day, time, and event. She can include her personal reflection, and her interpretation of the child's mood based on his expression. Encourage her to review these with the baby on a regular basis, even if he is an infant. As a baby, he will enjoy the close interaction and positive tone. Gradually he will come to understand the meaning as well as the intent of the activity. As her son grows, he will enjoy seeing himself at younger ages. It will give him concrete evidence of his physical growth and changing abilities.

MORE ACTIVITIES Use the photos to help the child learn about time by sequencing what he thinks came first, next and last. For the two year old, start with two photos, one as an infant and the other more current. Add more pictures as he gets older.

As mother and son look at the pictures, she can share how happy she was with him. She can tell him how she anticipated the events that would follow, such as first visitors and his first birthday party.

Photos can also be used to help her child feel close to grandparents, cousins, other relatives, or close friends who live far away.

ENDING THE ACTIVITY Always watch for signs of weariness and stop the activity when the child gets tired of it. Express pleasure and delight in spending the time with him. If strong feelings, negative moods, or anger have been discussed, reassure him that these feelings are okay, but express your confidence that problems can be resolved in peaceful ways. Reassure him that you will always be available to help him resolve conflicts, and that you will always love him even when he might have negative feelings. Tell your son that the photos will be kept in a safe place to be looked at again and again.

DEVELOPMENTAL INFORMATION

Photographs of children are a good way to show their developmental progress. They can also be used to help children think about times they reacted to experiences and events with joy or pleasure, or sadness and anger. Showing photographs to children over time helps them sequence their own growth process. Along with journals and letters, photos help children chronicle their own personal history.

DEVELOPMENTAL TEACHING

Share the above information with the mother. Encourage her to talk about her own childhood, what she remembers, what pleased her and what made her sad or angry. Help her identify the many moods she sees in her own baby, and how her son expresses them. Discuss ways that photographs will help her share these experiences and events with him. Discuss the importance of a family history and what it means to each member of the family. Encourage her to create a picture journal for her baby so they have a document portraying their own personal history.

Bitten

*You cannot
shake hands with
a clenched fist.*

- Indira Gandhi

GOAL The child will develop the ability to follow direction and accept limits.

AGE Birth to 36 months

PURPOSE To explore with parents the reasons children bite at different ages, and some ways of coping with this behavior.

ACTIVITY When the baby is teething, provide comforting objects for her to bite. Soft chewable toys, frozen pops or carrots, depending on the baby's age, might work. Teething rings and hard crunchy foods also might help. The mother can certainly show surprise and displeasure at being bitten, even if the bite was unintended. She can say, "Biting hurts." The reaction should not be harsh and never cause pain or humiliation for her child.

MORE ACTIVITIES When a toddler bites because of conflict or frustration, the mother can set firm limits, and encourage her daughter to use words, even if it is a simple "no," or "mine." The toddler can then be directed to activities like tearing or cutting paper, or making simple puppets with mouths that move. Such activities are described elsewhere in this document. **(See "Tearing Paper,"** pg. 103 **and "Make It Bite,"** pg. 105)

ENDING THE ACTIVITY Remind the mother to end with some sort of resolution. She can describe the behavior, reactions, and outcomes surrounding the biting. The mother needs to reassure her child that she has the ability to change inappropriate behavior. The mother should give reassurance that she loves her daughter and will always be available to her.

DEVELOPMENTAL INFORMATION

Children bite for a variety of reasons. Babies bite usually because they are teething, and chomping or biting down on something makes the gums feel better. Infants also tend to put objects in their mouths to learn about them. Part of this exploration is sucking and biting. In this case biting reflects an active exploration, a good phase of development, yet painful if done to a human object. Toddlers generally bite when they feel frustrated and don't have words to express how they feel. They also bite because they can't tell the difference between affection and aggression, and they are not always clear about body boundaries. Older toddlers and preschoolers might bite when angry, and sometimes do so because they want to hurt others.

SUGGESTED BOOKS

Baby Faces	Margaret Miller (Simon & Schuster, 1998)
Happy Days	Margaret Miller (Simon & Schuster, 1996)
Everywhere Babies	Susan Meyers (Harcourt , 2001)
No Biting!	Karen Katz (Grosset & Dunlap, 2002)

DEVELOPMENTAL TEACHING

Share the above information with the mother. Explore her feelings about biting. Usually adults become very angry with biters, and punish them, often by banishing. Help the mother learn ways to deal with biting that preserves the integrity and worth of her child, yet still deals with her own feelings about biting. Biting is a primitive behavior and brings out raw, primitive feelings in adults.

Baby's Story

GOAL   The child will develop the ability to play, pretend, and use symbols.

AGE   Birth to 12 months

PURPOSE   To help parents understand that babies think and feel even at this young age.

ACTIVITY   The baby should be held facing his mother and making eye contact. The mother tells her baby's story by describing what is happening, saying, "You are lying here just looking around". Encourage her to describe what her baby's inner state might be from his expressions. ("I bet you would like to say, 'My tummy is full. I think I'll take a nap.' ") Encourage the mother to make the story consistent with what the baby is doing. She wouldn't say anything about naps unless it was her baby's nap time.

MORE ACTIVITIES   Encourage the mother to use this activity when she and her baby are together. For example, while her baby is in the kitchen, she could describe his watching her cook. She could also describe what's happening. If the activity involves the baby, like getting his bottle ready, her story will be easy to tell.

Encourage the mother to talk to her baby during routines: feeding, diapering, playing, bathing, waking up, and going to bed. When feeding her baby she could say, "Oh, (name) really likes this kind of cereal. It's called rice cereal and it helps (baby's name) to grow." When changing a diaper the mother could say, "Now you are nice and dry, and it feels so good. I like taking care of you."

ENDING THE ACTIVITY   Encourage the mother to greet and leave her baby by using social conventions. When she approaches her baby she could say, "Hi, (name), mommy's here. I'm going to pick you up now." When leaving, she could say, "Mommy's going to get your bottle. I'll be right back."

DEVELOPMENTAL INFORMATION
During the early months of life, babies develop an awareness of external people and events by the contact they have with significant persons. When babies are held and have opportunities to interact with others, they are better able to shift their internal focus to awareness of the outer world.

DEVELOPMENTAL TEACHING
Help the mother turn her attention to her baby and help her observe her baby's various unique behaviors. Facial expressions are often overlooked at this age when many adults think babies are somewhat without personalities. The mother might feel that she only needs to respond to cries. The more that the mother is able to differentiate her baby's moods and needs, the more solid will be the attachment between them.

Sights and Sounds

GOAL The child will develop the ability to play, pretend, and use symbols.

AGE Birth to 3 months

PURPOSE To help babies develop eye muscles and listening ability. This activity helps babies move from an internal focus to an engagement with objects and people in the external world. Development at this age has to be mediated through a consistent adult caregiver.

ACTIVITY Encourage the father to carry his baby around, pointing out and naming objects or people they encounter. For example, "Here's Aunt Jo. She's come to visit us," or, "Oh, look, here's a ball. Balls are round and they roll. Let's give it a push." Continue in this fashion with other people and objects. Encourage the father to talk about the sounds that might go along with the sights. He could say, "I hear a bird singing. Look! There's the bird, and you can hear its song." Watch for babies' signals that they are tiring of the game.

MORE ACTIVITIES Encourage the father to point out objects by category, such as toys, furniture, or pictures in his baby's room.

As the baby gets older, the father can get down on the floor and crawl with her, looking under and over objects. This activity is not to teach the baby specific facts, but to lay the foundation upon which learning is built.

Tour the house with the baby, and take photos of the objects being shown. As his daughter gets older, the father can show her the real object and a photo of the object.

Be alert to cues about what's being looked at. Comment about what both father and child are seeing and hearing. For example, "You're looking at the dog. Do you see him wagging his tail? Can you hear him bark? I think he's saying, 'Woof woof!'"

Help the father make a mobile by cutting out black and white designs from newspapers, pictures in magazines or shapes from construction paper. If the father has a computer, he can make designs on that. These designs can be threaded on sturdy twine and hung from padded hangers.

ENDING THE ACTIVITY Watch for signs of weariness with the activity. When moving to something else, make a comment and say with expression, for example, "That was fun, but you look like you're tired." Talk about the good time you had playing and talking together. Tell what will happen next. Give your child a reassuring hug or pat.

DEVELOPMENTAL INFORMATION

In their initial weeks of life, babies are not very aware of their parents and other adult caregivers as individuals who nurture them. But as their needs are consistently met they begin to notice people and things in the world around them. During this same period the babies' vision is not very well developed. They can't focus very well, and they do not see with the clarity they will have later. Babies also sleep a lot. When they are awake they need something interesting to see and hear. Most interesting are the adult caregivers and their voices talking or singing to the babies. Parents and other caregivers can make this world interesting to babies by engaging them in activities, showing objects, and talking to them. **Learning to listen at this time sets the stage for later attentiveness.**

DEVELOPMENTAL TEACHING

Share the above information with the father. Encourage him to interact with his daughter and engage her in observing her surroundings. The father should think of himself as a tour guide and talk to his baby about what she sees and hears in the environment. The focus should be on sights, sounds, actions, and the relationship among these. The father can also talk about the baby's reactions to what's happening around them. For example, he could say, "Oops! That loud noise startled you."

Peek-a-Boo

GOAL   The child will develop the ability to play, pretend, and use symbols.

AGE   Birth to 12 months

PURPOSE   To engage children in symbolic or pretend play, such as "appearing and disappearing". These activities can set the stage for talking about pretending and play with parents.

ACTIVITY   When the mother notices her baby watching her, she can hide her face behind her hands for a short period of time, then lift her hands and say "Peek-a-boo." As her baby gets older, the mother can hide in one place and pop-up in another. She can extend the amount of time hidden before popping up, or she can hide under a blanket or behind a piece of furniture and pop up to surprise him, saying, "Peek-a-boo" in a quiet calm voice. This creates a little tension in the baby, so the mother needs to make sure that she does not wait too long, or pop-up too unexpectedly or with too much excitement. She should watch her baby carefully to notice if he seems uncomfortable with the game. She should stop if he shows distress and quickly give reassurance of her presence and care.

MORE ACTIVITIES   This play can be extended to toys and having baby look for them. Ask, "Where's the rattle?" When the baby lifts the cover, say excitedly, "There it is." Babies under the age of eight or nine months may not look for the object at first. By eight months, they will usually look for it in the spot it was before it was hidden. When they are a little older, babies will be able to search for objects until they find them.

ENDING THE ACTIVITY   End with a positive embrace and a reassurance that mommy will always be around to care for her baby, and when mommy goes away, she will always come back.

DEVELOPMENTAL INFORMATION

From the time they are about one month old, babies tune into the presence of parents and follow them when they are in the line of sight. Babies sometimes think that the returning parent is a new one. Babies gradually learn about the permanence of people by having many experiences with their comings and goings. After five months of age, babies have some beginning awareness of the constancy of the reappearing parent, but still fear, at some level, a final disappearance. This game helps babies deal with their fear of disappearance, the pleasure of reappearance, and helps them develop a loving relationship with a permanent parent. This playful experience helps babies feel in control, and enables them to master separation.

DEVELOPMENTAL TEACHING

Share the above information with the mother. Ask her to talk to her baby when she observes his eyes following her. This will help her baby associate the mother's voice with her physical image. Explain to the mother that activities such as these help her baby to pretend and later to engage in symbolic and abstract activities which foster learning.

Your Turn, My Turn

For news of the heart, ask the face.
- Hausa Proverb

GOAL The child will develop the ability to be a responsive partner and engage in pro-social behavior.

AGE 3 to 12 months

PURPOSE To develop language interaction between parents and their babies, and to set the stage for learning about social conversation. This activity also promotes language development when babies see they are effective in getting their parent's attention.

ACTIVITY The baby and mother should be about eight to twelve inches apart, facing each other. In this activity the mother lets her baby take the lead or first turn in vocalizing. This will work best when the baby is alert and comfortable, after feeding or diapering, for example. Following along, the mother imitates her daughter's sounds or vocalizations. The mother can also tell her baby that she has noticed that her baby wants to communicate, and she is responding by "talking back".

MORE ACTIVITIES The mother can repeat her baby's sounds. She can then vocalize a different sound that her baby has made earlier. The mother can also comment on the sounds her baby is making, describing how they are different and how the sounds relate to the baby's mood.

The song, **"When you're happy and you know it clap your hands,"** can be used with different words to label the child's mood. (excited-wave your arms)

ENDING THE ACTIVITY Encourage the mother to notice when her baby is ready to go on to something else. Suggest that she make a closing statement, such as, "It looks like you're finished talking." The mother can also comment on what the baby seemed to be trying to communicate. For example, she might say, "You had lots to say. You seemed happy," or, "You made a sad face when you said [repeat sound]."

DEVELOPMENTAL INFORMATION

Babies learn language best in social interactions. It is helpful when the mother responds to her infant's sounds, recognizing them as the earliest acquisition of both language and communication. The mother can promote this development by allowing her baby to take the lead. As the baby gets older, the mother can then extend the language by supplying other sounds and words. The baby might make her first random sounds simply because she can. When the mother responds to those sounds, repeats them, and then gives back new and different sounds, it shows her baby that the communication skill is useful. The baby will use new sounds to keep her mother engaged or to get her attention.

DEVELOPMENTAL TEACHING

Share the above information with the mother. Talk about the different ways her family communicates, especially non-verbally. Discuss how those non-verbal communications were developed, and how meaningful they are to the relationships. Have the mother focus on her baby and establish communication. This differs from the activity "My Turn, Your Turn" because the mother watches for her baby to make the first move. Thus, this activity also encourages the mother to observe her baby's behavior.

Run and Chase

GOAL The child will develop the ability to be a responsive partner and engage in pro-social behavior.

AGE 6 to 24 months

PURPOSE To help children deal with and practice separations, giving them the opportunity to control or take charge of separations. This activity engages parents and children in a game that represents the comings and goings, or the children's moving away and then reuniting with the parents.

ACTIVITY Encourage the father to initiate the game by his getting down on hands and knees and making an inviting statement such as "I'm going to catch you" while moving towards the child. This should be said in a playful and non-threatening way. The child will probably respond by running. If not, the father can "catch" or reunite with the child, saying something like, "Now I've got you". The father can then invite the child to catch him. Usually, by this time, the child catches on and engages in playing the game.

MORE ACTIVITIES Sometimes the father might feel silly crawling around, and the Home Visitor may have to be the initiator of the game, encouraging the father to take over and continue the game with the child.

Encourage the father to establish rituals or routines around separations, however brief. The father can encourage his child to say, "I'll be back, daddy," before leaving the room, and he can respond with, "I'll be here when you come back." This exchange helps in separating.

Encourage the parents to read books such as the **Runaway Bunny** and **How Much Do I Love You?** along with playing the game described in the story, a kind of reenactment of **Runaway Bunny.**

Another game has the father and child on their hands and knees. As the baby starts to crawl away the father teasingly says, "Oh, no you don't," and gently pulls on his legs to keep him close. Sometimes the father lets him get away. This game shares power between the father and child, yet gives the child a sense of security about the availability of his father.

This activity can also be modified for use with a baby who has learned to crawl. Encourage the father to describe what is happening, He could say, "You're crawling away from me, but I'm going to get you." Encourage the father to gauge when the child might be over-stimulated, weary of the game, or frightened by the intense physical actions.

ENDING THE ACTIVITY The father can say something about enjoying the activity and reaffirming his availability to his son. He can tell the baby what is going to happen next. For example, "You can play with this toy," handing the baby a toy, or, "Now it's time for lunch. You can stay here and play with your toys while I get your bottle ready."

DEVELOPMENTAL INFORMATION

At the end of the first year, children are gaining new feelings of independence. Some are walking and can freely move away from the parent. If they can't walk, they "cruise" or crawl, or in some fashion show control over their own mobility. They explore away from the immediate area of the parent. While children take great pride in this ability, they are still concerned about their parent's availability for reunion when the explorations are over. Some children love to "run away" from the parent, taking special delight in being "caught". They enjoy watching the parent take a turn at running and being caught. This symbolic leaving and reuniting helps children feel in control as they "catch" the parent, and feel reassured as they are also "caught".

Many children shadow their parent and get underfoot, refusing to go out and explore on their own. Games such as this help children move toward independent behavior in their environment as they realize that their parent can be available, even at a distance. They come to realize that they will not be abandoned by the parent as they become more competent, nor will the parent allow them to get out of control as they move around and explore their environment.

SUGGESTED READING

Peekaboo Morning   Rachel Isadora (G.P. Putnam's Sons, 2002)

Babies on the Move   Susan Canizares (Scholastic, Inc.)

We must not, in trying to think about how
we can make a big difference,
ignore the small daily differences
we can make which, over time,
add up to big differences that we
often cannot foresee.

- Marian Wright Edelman

DEVELOPMENTAL TEACHING

Encourage the father to think about the ways he communicates his availability to his child. Talk about making eye contact from a distance, or talking to his son from a distance or just by watching and listening. The child will feel more secure in beginning to explore and moving away from the immediate vicinity of his father if he is confident that his father will be available when he returns. A father who has been consistent and responsive to the needs of his baby will have an easier time in encouraging his child's independence and exploration. The condition of having needs met is necessary for the child's developing competence as he gets older.

Help him child-proof his home so his child can feel comfortable in moving away, and the father can feel comfortable that he doesn't always have to be hovering over his son. Help the father reinforce his child's independence by acknowledging his explorations and showing delight in their reunions.

My Body, My Body

DEVELOPMENTAL TEACHING
Share the above information with the mother. Talk with her about ways that this activity helps her daughter develop an awareness of her own body and how it will aid in her self-concept. This awareness sets the stage for the baby's learning about what each part of the body can do and creates a foundation for developing competence and self-esteem. Ask the mother about games she already knows, particularly those she might have played as a child with a significant adult. Encourage her to think about some games that were specific to her family or culture.

GOAL   The child will develop the ability to be a responsive partner and show pro-social behavior.

AGE   3 to 18 months

PURPOSE   To engage baby in pleasurable activities that show an understanding of the baby as a competent being who can learn and who is fun to play with.

ACTIVITY   When the baby is in an alert stage and seems ready for play, introduce a game such as **Patty-Cake** p.154. Start the game and do the movements for the baby if necessary. Describe the action by saying, "We're playing patty-cake. You put your hands together like this." Then proceed with the rhyme. Do a similar activity with **This Little Piggy** p. 153 and other games remembered from childhood.

MORE ACTIVITIES   As the baby gets older and has good upper body control, the mother can introduce knee games. Placing her baby on her knees, the mother can rock her baby gently while holding her and reciting the rhymes.

Ride A Horsie
Horsie, horsie, riding along
Hits a bump, whoo, whoo!
Horsie, horsie riding along
Hits a bump, whoa!

Trot, Trot to Boston
Trot, trot to Boston town
To get a stick of candy.
One for you and one for me
And one for Dicky Dandy

Babies will begin to initiate some of these activities. For example, the baby might start to rock or bounce as soon as she is placed on her mother's lap. When her baby starts the game, the mother should respond by continuing the game, thus acknowledging her baby's ability to guide the interaction. Encourage the mother to think of times when they might naturally play these games, as during bedtime or while changing diapers.

This is also a good time for the mother to exercise the baby's arms and legs gently, talking about different parts of the body as she diapers her baby. The mother can play a game such as, **Where Is Baby's Nose?** and help her baby find her nose. The game repeats with 'mommy's nose', and can continue with eyes, mouth, and ears.

ENDING THE ACTIVITY   The mother should watch for signs that the baby has grown tired of the game. She can tell her baby what she noticed about her response, such as "You're laughing. You must think this is fun," or, "I think you are getting tired. We'll stop now." The mother might add that she enjoyed the game, also.

Conversations - Beginning the Dialogue

GOAL The child will develop the ability to be a responsive partner and engage in pro-social behavior.

AGE Birth to 36 months

PURPOSE For babies and young children to develop a sense of self as communicators and as partners in dialogue.

ACTIVITY Encourage the mother to talk to her baby when they are together and he is awake. Meaningful conversations occur when the mother describes what she is doing with her baby, like changing his diaper, feeding or dressing him.

Encourage her to discuss what she sees the baby doing and what he seems to be feeling. For example, "You're kicking your arms and legs so much. You must be very excited (or happy.)" The mother can also describe what they are both doing, such as, "You are really watching mommy. I'm cooking your lunch (or doing the wash)." She can describe what the baby is hearing or seeing by saying, "Oh, you heard that noise. That is the man coming to pick up the garbage." She can also take the baby to the source of the sound, or closer to the object being examined.

MORE ACTIVITIES As her baby grows older, the mother can describe his attempts to make sounds, saying for example, "You're moving your mouth, I think you're trying to say something." When her baby does make sounds, she should respond and act as though his sounds were intended to mean something. She might say, "You're trying to tell me you're hungry (or wet)." "Your sounds tell me you're starting to talk to me." "You're happy.... you're watching that toy."

When the baby's gestures, sounds or beginning words do communicate an intent, the mother should respond to it. When her baby points to a cookie she might say, "You want a cookie. Just a minute and I'll get you one. Here it is. Can you say cookie?" Don't expect a response right away, but responding in this way anticipates that the baby will eventually respond.

For variety, the mother can sing some of her conversations.

It is helpful to take photographs. When the baby is older, the mother can talk with him about the event depicted in the photo and his relation to it. For example, "Here is a picture of you when you started to crawl. We were all so excited."

ENDING THE ACTIVITY Be alert so that the baby is not over-stimulated or over-tired. Let him know how pleased you are at his response and how much fun the game was. Remind him of what happens next.

DEVELOPMENTAL INFORMATION

Most babies are born with all that they need to be responsive to the environment. It is up to the adults to make sure babies are stimulated so that they want to interact with the people and objects they encounter. Talking with babies is one important way to let them know the world is filled with caring persons and interesting objects. Talking with babies and young children also provides a good model for language development and encourages children to talk back in turn. Babies should be talked to most of the time when they are awake and alert. They should not be forced to respond, but can be encouraged by being talked to in varied voice tones, being sung to, or being shown interesting objects.

DEVELOPMENTAL TEACHING

Share the above information with the mother. Review the stages of language development. Some adults feel silly talking to a baby who isn't yet verbal. Explain that language experiences relate to later success in learning to read and write. Remind them that a baby has to have the words or tools of language, and they also have to experience the uses of language. Adults model these for infants by talking with them. Language is also a social activity, and it makes the baby feel that there are people around who care.

Index to Activities: 12-24 months

Conversations - Now You are One

If we want to survive, we must love our children more than we hate our enemies.

\- Irene Brown

DEVELOPMENTAL INFORMATION

There are certain important milestones that occur around 12-24 months that move children into a more independent position. In addition to learning to walk, they improve their fine motor skills and manage toys more creatively. They are beginning to use language to communicate and express their own desires, including the word "no". They also have the ability to understand directives. Children begin to act with intent, not just in response to a stimulus or a need. Parents sometimes see these intentional acts as being directed toward them. If the child's behavior is negative, such as hitting out, the parents may retaliate. The child's newly developing ability to deny others and say "No" is seen as purposely defiant. Parents might have feelings about the child's growing independence and ability to "leave" the parent and get around on her own. This developing sense of self might be discomforting to the parent and result in relational conflict.

GOAL The child will develop a sense of body self and self-regulation.

AGE 12 to 24 months

PURPOSE To get parents to focus on the positive aspect of their child's emerging self-development, especially the approaching sense of autonomy. This activity might generate issues parents might have with the child's increasing separateness and impending struggle for independence.

ACTIVITY It is important to find a time when the father seems happy with his child. Suggest that the father hold his daughter cradled snugly on his lap. Have the father look into his child's eyes and talk to her. The conversation should focus around the baby's development during her first year and the change from a dependent baby to a more separate, increasingly independent one. Help the father identify the milestones his child has achieved to the current time, and how he feels about them. If the father has photographs of the baby, they can be used for this discussion. Encourage the father to share the photos with his child (e.g., "When you were one month old you slept most of the time," or, "When you first ate (food name) you spit it in my face, but you loved (food name)."

The father continues this review, adding his feelings about the baby's growth (e.g., "It was exciting to see you begin to crawl, say your first word, say ma, da.") It is all right if the father shares some negative reactions (e.g., food spit in his face) as long as his feelings are not obvious or expressed with an angry voice. Ask the father to talk about things he would like his child to know. Discuss how the parent-child conversations have changed since earlier exchanges. The father could comment on his changing hopes and dreams, and changes in their family life.

MORE ACTIVITIES Keep a journal or write to the child about these changes in letter form. It can be dictated, written down, and then returned for the memory book. If possible, take a monthly photograph of the child. Paste this picture in the journal or scrapbook, along with the written conversation. These memorabilia can also be stored in a box.

ENDING THE ACTIVITY End on a positive note with regard to the baby's development. Give your daughter a comforting touch, pat, or hug.

SUGGESTED READING

What Can You Do in the Sun?   Anna Grossnicle Hines (Greenwillow, 1999)

Baby High, Baby Low   Stella Blackstone (Barefoot Books, 1997)

Wake Up, Me!   Marnie McGee (Simon & Schuster, 2002)

I dream of giving birth
to a child who will ask:
"Mother, what is war?"

- Eve Merriam

DEVELOPMENTAL TEACHING

Share the above information with the father. This activity will elicit developmental information about his child's emerging abilities, especially those around her sense of self and ability to act more independently. It might also give staff clues about the father's feelings regarding his child's ability to act with intention and independence. It can indicate a need for staff to provide developmental support to promote stronger bonds between the father and child.

GOAL The child will develop the ability to follow directions and accept limits.

AGE 18 to 36 months

SITUATION Visiting with Mrs. Kallan, the Home Visitor suggests giving 18-month-old Jamal more choices. The mother says she does give him choices, sometimes. She adds that at meal time she used to ask him if he wanted to eat, but he always said, "No." The mother doesn't ask him any more, but just tells him it's time to eat. He usually says "No," and when she insists he come to the table, he ends up having a temper tantrum.

WHAT TO TELL THE PARENT There are two issues here: one is eating, about which Jamal has limited choices, and the other is the 'no' as a demonstration of defiance. Sometimes parents focus on the wrong issue when children say 'no' to them. They focus on the defiance or non-compliance and get into control struggles. If parents ignore the 'no' and just move on with the activity, the child will usually comply.

Eating. Children can be given all kinds of choices, depending on their family style and routine. It is not unusual for 18 month old children to still be on their own time schedule. If that is the case, it makes sense for the mother to ask Jamal if he is hungry and is ready to eat. He will most likely say yes and eat when he is hungry. The Home Visitor can discuss with the mother the types of food being offered. When children are still on their own schedule, it might be harder to monitor eating between meals, which may interfere with the child's eating at meal time.

Sometimes the child will say 'no' but will still follow physical directions to sit at the table and eat; he will allow himself to be placed in his high chair. In such cases, the mother should just ignore the 'no', and proceed with the mealtime routine.

Non-compliance Sometimes it is saying 'no' that is upsetting because the mother sees it as defiance of her authority or as the child's rejection of her nurturing efforts. Responsibility for oneself is a desirable attribute. Nevertheless, this can be a trying time for a parent. Better motor ability, combined with curiosity and lack of experience, make adult monitoring essential. The result may be a battle of wills between parent and child. It is important for both to express their temporary negative feelings in acceptable ways. The mother can use verbal expressions; her son will need an appropriate way to act out his feelings.

Avoid using "want" questions unless the mother is prepared to give her child a true choice. For example, "Do you want to go to bed?" when she really means, "It's time to go to bed."

As the striving for independence is successfully resolved, the child achieves a stronger sense of competence to manage himself and to deal with the world.

DEVELOPMENTAL INFORMATION
At this age the baby's struggle for independence is hard to overlook. The ability and desire to do for himself reflects his developing sense of self. It is based on the security of his relationship with his parents and his wish to imitate them. Thus, he tries to feed himself or take charge of his bath. Such efforts are facilitated by the baby's growing motor skills and control of his body. He is learning that his mother is not always going to be around to do his bidding and he struggles to assert some independence.

He also wishes to assume some of the control others have over him. To equalize the power with adults, he says 'no', just as he hears his mother often saying 'no' to him. Sometimes he may have a tendency to say 'no' to everything, even when he really wants to do whatever is being suggested. It is important to help the mother distinguish between his saying 'no' for its own sake and saying 'no' as non-compliance.

WHAT THE PARENT CAN DO The mother can limit snacking and can designate a certain time for meals. If the mother wants to give choices and if she designates mealtime at a certain hour, she can give the child a choice between two items. An example might be between a peanut butter or cheese sandwich, or soup and chicken fingers. In this instance she avoids the opportunity for Jamal to say 'no'. The mother can give choices that are closed-ended, a choice between two types of food. Avoid asking questions such as "What do you want for lunch?" especially when it might not be possible to honor a particular request.

Add some humor. For example, say, "What am I going to do with my no, no, boy?" This should be said lightly, with a touch of humor, perhaps while giving the child an affectionate pat on his back, or a little hug.

ENDING THE ACTIVITY Reinforce good food choices by saying, "You're starting to make choices that will make you healthy."

Our earth is but a small star
in the great universe, yet of it
we can make, if we choose,
a planet unvexed by war,
untroubled by hunger or fear,
undivided by senseless
distinctions of race, color, or theory.
                                    - Stephen Vincent Benet

Coffee Can Drop

GOAL   The child will develop an understanding of how things work and how to make things happen.

AGE   12 to 36 months

PURPOSE   To help babies develop a sense of accomplishment and of making an impact on the environment, giving them a feeling of success or mastery.

DEVELOPMENTAL INFORMATION

Toward the end of the first year, children have the ability to move around and that allows them to play apart from their mothers. They will manage this task better when they see themselves as competent and effective. Being able to do things on their own, however simple, will help them feel they can impact their world. These feelings will be even more intense if children are able to get the mother to pay attention to them when they need her. When they see an object disappear from the coffee can and then reappear when the lid is off, they learn that things out of sight still exist. Later they transfer that learning to their mother's leaving, realizing that she still is around even when they cannot see her. This activity will help children learn about the nature of objects when they have to turn the clothes pins to fit in more tailored holes.

ACTIVITY   Make sure the container is safe and has no sharp edges. Cut a hole in the plastic lid and give the child a variety of objects to drop in the hole. For the younger child around one year old, the mother could cut a large hole in the center of the can and give her daughter objects to drop into the hole. The objects should be safe and fit the guidelines for safe size. Large sewing spools, small blocks, or clothes pins are generally appropriate.

After the child drops the objects into the hole, she can take the lid off and dump them out. The mother can replace the lid and start the game again. If the child protests putting the lid back on, that is all right. Just let the child drop the object directly into the container. This might be a way to start the game so her child can see the object dropping into the can, and learn to turn the container over to get it out.

MORE ACTIVITIES   As the baby grows older, the mother can change this activity. For example, she can cut the hole to match more closely the objects to be dropped. She can also cut several holes similar in shape to the objects, such as a square hole for the small block, a round hole for the spool, and a smaller round hole for the clothespin. This will provide a challenge for the child who will have to learn to maneuver the object to make it fit. The mother can also choose objects that make different sounds when dropped. She can identify the object, sound, and talk about how it sounds different from the other objects.

ENDING THE ACTIVITY   Every activity should have a verbal warning that it is ending. The child will probably end this game on her own. However, if it must be ended before she tires of it, say something like, "One more time and then we will put the toy away." Again, tell the child what is going to happen next.

DEVELOPMENTAL TEACHING

Share the above information with the mother. The Home Visitor can help her make this activity fun, rather than drilling the baby to perform this task in a school-like manner. This activity can be created using materials available in the home. The Home Visitor can help make this game by using a coffee can or any container that is safe and has a plastic lid. Some bread crumbs, stuffing, oatmeal, cream cheese or margarine come in containers that can be used for this activity.

Cooking Eggs

18-36 mo.

GOAL   The child will develop an understanding of how things work and how to make things happen.

AGE   18 to 36 months

PURPOSE   To help children learn about changes in food and to engage them in a grown-up activity. This will also give an opportunity to talk about nutrition with the parents.

ACTIVITY   Break an egg into a plastic bag and seal it tightly, making sure that air has been expelled. Let the child knead the bag to break up (scramble) the egg. As her son grows older he can use a fork and bowl or substitute a small whisk for the fork. When the egg is mixed, pour it into a skillet. An older child might be able to do this by himself, under careful supervision. Allow the child to watch the egg cook in order to observe the changes. This can be done while he is standing on a chair or sitting on the counter, far enough away from the stove for safety. Talk about how the egg changes in form.

MORE ACTIVITIES   Make Jello together. Allow the child to help pour the Jello, cold water, and ice into a bowl, mix and refrigerate to see the changes as the Jello sets.

Read a book together, or say a rhyme such as the following:

> 5 eggs and 5 eggs
> That makes ten
> Sitting on top is a mother hen
> Cheep, cheep, cheep, what do I see
> Ten yellow chicks as fluffy as can be

Make play dough to see how ingredients change when they are mixed together.

ENDING THE ACTIVITY   The mother might say, "It's fun and interesting to make things change. We'll do it again another day."

DEVELOPMENTAL TEACHING

Share the above information with the mother. Ask her to think about times her child showed surprise when the mother looked different. Help her talk about changes as she helps the child with each part of the activity. The Home Visitor can also use this time to talk with the mother about nutritional foods and snacks.

This activity gives an opportunity for mother and son to show nurturing behavior toward each other as they cook and eat together. Participating in this kind of "grown-up" activity also gives the young child a sense of power that makes him feel good.

Toy Toss

GOAL   The child will develop trust through secure attachments and meaningful relationships.

AGE   12 to 36 months

PURPOSE   To provide the opportunity for parents to develop social interactions with baby around a common task or expectation. This will allow parents to engage with young children using a game-like approach to clean-up. When the child is of preschool age, parents can generally expect the child to put toys away.

ACTIVITY   After a toddler has been playing awhile and there is an assortment of toys scattered about the floor the father can invite him to pick up the toys. Make a game of it by asking him to place or toss (if safe) toys into a small basket, box, bucket, coffee can, laundry basket, or blanket. When the child participates, the father should show pleasure by smiling, praising, and commenting on the child's behavior and accomplishment. He might even sing the Barney clean-up song, some other song, or make one up about putting toys away.

The Clean Up Song
Clean up, clean up, everybody everywhere.
Clean up, clean up, everybody do your share.

This activity should not be seen as part of a serious clean-up, nor should the child be given responsibility for all of the toys. The object here is to have fun, so the father should avoid engaging in power struggles with his son. The interaction should be playful with some opportunity for control given to the child. He may gather the toys only to dump them out again, and start the task all over again. The father should plan for some time to allow this dumping and filling, stopping on the filling cycle.

MORE ACTIVITIES   Fathers can make storage spaces for older children with a picture or symbol of the toy that should be placed there. Small plastic containers allow for sorting, making this a learning activity. Around three years of age, children can be given a clean-up task as part of their family responsibility. If the child marks a surface with crayon or marker, provide a wet sponge or washcloth. The child will enjoy wiping the surface clean.

If the father is uncomfortable with messes, he can use charts or posters to aid the child in keeping focused on the task. He should leave messy clean-ups for himself or closely supervise the child who is assigned such tasks.

Make toy clean-up into a tossing game. Use plastic baskets as containers for plastic blocks, small animal figures, stuffed animals, etc. When it is time to clean up the toys, line up the baskets and make a game of tossing the blocks into the block basket, animals into the animal basket, and so on. This kind of constructive tossing can also be used to pick up dirty clothes, paper scraps, and sorting laundry.

DEVELOPMENTAL INFORMATION

This activity sets the stage for learning about responsibility for belongings and keeping some order in the home environment with regard to play. During preschool years, children are able to help restore a sense of order by putting toys away. At this young age, children can begin the activity of picking up toys by engaging with parents in a game-like activity.

DEVELOPMENTAL TEACHING

Help the father focus on ways he can have fun with his child during common household tasks such as cleaning-up. This activity makes a game out of picking up toys.

By 18 months of age most children can get around pretty well, and they have the ability to use fine motor skills to pick up objects. They are also able to understand language and love being involved with adults around adult activities. This activity takes advantage of these developmental capabilities.

As they approach the second year of life children are interested in doing and undoing tasks as they perform activities over and over, working and "un-working" puzzles, for example. This activity can build on that tendency. This activity also allows toddlers, working on controlling messes in toilet training, to undo the mess they have created and restore order.

CONTINUED

ENDING THE ACTIVITY   Praise the child for doing a good job of helping with the cleaning. Give the child a hug and explain what's coming next.

SUGGESTED BOOKS

Come Back, Hannah!   Marisabina Russo (Greenwillow Books, 2001)

Show Me!   Tom Tracy (Harper Festival)

There are two things of
*   lasting value we can give our children -*
one is roots, the other is wings.

- Anonymous

DEVELOPMENTAL TEACHING CONTINUED

As toddlers become more independent they take a great deal of pride in being able to accomplish small tasks and helping adults. They can use a wet sponge to wipe off tables or play areas.

72

We have not inherited the Earth from our ancestors.
We have only borrowed it from our children.
  - Ancient Proverb

GOAL   The child will develop trust through secure attachments and meaningful relationships.

AGE   12 to 36 months

PURPOSE   To help children deal with separations, in this case moving from one place to another. This activity gives children the opportunity to rehearse and control the separations and reunions which will help them cope with moving from one place to another. Examples are moving from home to day care, from one group to another in day care, or physically from one house to another. This activity provides a van, a U-Haul truck, or toy train for the child to use in pretending the moving operation.

ACTIVITY   Work with the parent to make a toy train by stringing together several milk cartons, cheese boxes, or small food boxes (rice, pudding, for example). Attach a long piece of yarn to the front of the "train" so the child can pull it along. Provide some small stuffed toys and other objects that can be used as train loads. Encourage the child to define two places and "move" from one to the other.

Plan with the mother how to encourage her daughter to act out her experience of moving. Her children will probably continue to play this game after the move. Plan what to say to the child about the move, finding the right balance of feeling about loss of the old and anticipation of the new. Again, the mother should focus on her own memories of similar experiences from her childhood.

DEVELOPMENTAL INFORMATION
During the first three years children are working on establishing a solid sense of self. This development occurs in relationship to meaningful adults, most notably the parents. As children grow they are sensitive to their parent's reactions, looking for affirmation of their abilities and "goodness". They are also dependent on parents for care and nurturing. Until they have a sense of competence, they tend to resist separation from their parents and are stressed when they are apart for long periods of time.

Because of this sensitivity to separation, children come to rely on possessions and the predictable nature of their environment to assure themselves that things stay the same. This constancy helps them cope with separations because some things don't change and they can keep control over some possessions.

CONTINUED

MORE ACTIVITIES   Help the mother find small cardboard boxes to use as "packing" crates and allow the child to "pack" up scrap objects. Encourage the child to use the cartons as play houses, setting up two different houses and moving from one to the other with all of the possessions. Encourage the mother to allow her child to pack some of their real belongings in small boxes or cloth bags that they can physically carry from the old to the new house.

Take a photograph of the current home, the child's bed, or a favorite place. Take a photo of the new home, the door, the bed, the living room, or a favorite friend. Help the child choose something to hang on a bed when they move.

Sing transportation songs such as **I've Been Working on the Railroad** or:

> **Engine, Engine # 9**
> Engine, Engine #9
> Going down the Chicago line
> If the train should jump the track
> Will I get my money back?
> Yes...no...Maybe so

Riding in a Wagon
Riding in a wagon
Riding in a wagon
Wheels go round and round
Riding in a wagon.

The Wheels on the Bus
The wheels on the bus go round and round,
Round and round, round and round.
The wheels on the bus go round and round,
All through the town.

The people on the bus go bump, bump, bump...
The horn on the bus goes toot, toot, toot...

ENDING THE ACTIVITY   The mother can say something about enjoying the activity and tell the child what is going to happen next. If the parent is stopping the activity, the child should be given advance notice that play time is over and given the chance to have one or two "last turns".

DEVELOPMENTAL INFORMATION CONTINUED

When children move from place to place too frequently, or when they move from one living space to another, the stability of their world comes into question and so does the constancy or everlasting presence of their parents. At times of environmental change it is helpful for children to be able to control some comings and goings if only symbolically. Children will engage in representational play when they are around 18 months of age. They then can use toys to recreate their experiences.

DEVELOPMENTAL TEACHING

Encourage the mother to think about her own early situations with regard to changes, going to stay with a relative, moving, or starting school.

Ask the mother to recall her feelings, fears, and concerns to help her develop a base of empathy for her daughter. Focus on things the mother did that helped her feel better about the situation, especially in using transition objects or other possessions. Recall how some adults were helpful (or not helpful). Encourage the mother to provide toys that will allow her child to anticipate the upcoming experience. Encourage her to talk to her child about the experience of change or moving.

What's Inside

GOAL The child will develop the ability to express feelings in appropriate ways.

AGE 12 to 36 months

PURPOSE To help children cope with feelings around separation. This activity allows children to recreate and control the appearance and disappearance of objects.

ACTIVITY The mother can provide nesting toys that fit inside one another or small plastic containers of different sizes. There are toys such as "Kitten in a keg" that are inexpensive and serve this purpose well. If the mother is using plastic containers, she might glue a small object to the bottom of the smallest container, making sure that the object is large enough so the child cannot swallow it. Allow the child to play with the toys when the mother is present. She can describe how the child is using the toy and talk about what's inside. When the small object is found, the mother can exclaim, "Oh, my! Look what you found inside!" If the mother can't find an appropriate object to glue, a piece of material would work, making sure that all ends are securely glued. As a substitute, make a mark with crayon in the bottom of the container. The idea is to have something inside that the child can uncover and cover up again.

MORE ACTIVITIES As the child gets older she can hide objects for her mother to find, and at a still older age she can hide herself from her mother (going away as the mother had done). The mother can also take a picture of herself with her child or she can give the child a small soft object to keep in a pocket for comfort in the mother's absence.

Read the book, Goodnight Moon. (See pgs. 3-4)

ENDING THE ACTIVITY The mother can point out that the object is always there (always comes back), just as the parent is always there, although sometimes away (hiding or being covered) for a short period. The mother can reinforce that she always comes back. Give a reassuring touch, hug, or pat.

DEVELOPMENTAL INFORMATION

Near the end of the first year, babies become aware that parents can leave and some children begin to cry when that happens. At about 18 months toddlers have renewed concerns with separation and parents' leaving as they try to control the availability and closeness of significant adults. While they know that objects and people continue to exist even when not visible, they do not yet have a secure sense of self as competent enough to get along when caregivers are not immediately available. Being able to control the appearance and disappearance of objects helps them cope when parents leave or are out of sight.

DEVELOPMENTAL TEACHING

Encourage the mother to provide toys that her child can hide. Discuss the mother's feelings and concerns about separations, how she experienced these as a child, and how she may have used toys and adults to help herself feel better. Separation can be painful for children. Parents also experience the pain but in a different way. There is a tendency to tell the child to "Be big," "Don't cry," or minimize the child's feelings.
Encourage the mother to allow her child to protest her leaving, but to provide toys and activities that will help her master these experiences.

Toddling and Falling

GOAL The child will develop the ability to follow directions and accept limits.

AGE 12 to 24 months

PURPOSE To help children make a game of knocking over objects or building blocks. Children will be able to see the effects of their actions.

ACTIVITY Provide musical balls or other toys that have been weighted so they return to their upright position even after being knocked over, small light weight blocks, or nesting cups. The father can demonstrate the action of the toy, or help stack the blocks for the very young child. Encourage the child to knock over the toy or to make a stack of blocks and then knock them over. A stack of two to four high is probably a good number for this age. The child might tire of this game after three to five repetitions.

NOTE: The father can make light weight blocks out of small pint or half-pint milk containers.

MORE ACTIVITIES As his child gets older the father can encourage him to see how high he can stack the blocks. That activity gives the added dimension of learning about balance.

Sing a song such as:

The Noble Duke of York
The noble Duke of York,
He had ten thousand men.
He led them up the hill,
And then back down again.

And when you're up, you're up.
And when you're down, you're down.
And when you're in between,
You're neither up nor down.

Or play:

Ring Around The Rosy
Ring around the rosy,
Pocket full of posies,
Ashes, ashes,
We all fall down.

ENDING THE ACTIVITY Have the father describe what the child did to the toy and what happened. Make the connection between the toy's action and self action, saying, for example, "Oh, look, it fell over and got back up, just like when you fall and get back up." Give the child a comforting touch or hug and add, "And daddy is here to help you when you need it."

DEVELOPMENTAL INFORMATION
Before 12 months of age children are beginning to explore upright mobility. During these times, when they are sitting upright or starting to stand they tend to topple over from time to time. These falls, while usually not harmful, can cause children to become fearful when they are unable to control their bodies. This activity allows the child to use toys that move through space. Parents can provide musical toys and small toys with rounded bottoms (small versions of BOBO dolls) that children can push over, but which right themselves. Blocks or boxes that can be stacked, knocked over and stacked again can also be used. These toys allow children to mirror their own actions and control them through play. This activity is related to the child's falling over and getting back up.

DEVELOPMENTAL TEACHING
Encourage the father to provide toys that represent falling and getting up again. Discuss the father's attitude about walking and the independence it brings. Some fathers push their children to walk early and encourage them to stand even when their muscles cannot support the weight. The Home Visitor can use this time to discuss appropriate ways to encourage a child to walk. This is also a time to introduce "setting boundaries" by cueing the child, "You can stop at the door. I'll watch."

Pushing Buttons

GOAL	The child will develop the ability to follow directions and accept limits.
AGE	18 to 36 months

Parenting is not a skill. It is a relationship.
— Unknown

SITUATION   Jillene, 20 months old, pushes the buttons on the television set. Her mother tells her firmly, "No," and redirects her to play with her toy radio which plays music and shows pictures. Jillene returns to the TV. Her mother holds her hands and stops her, saying, "No." She picks her up and takes her into her bedroom. She gets a storybook and says, "Let's read a story," as she sits on the floor with Jillene snuggled onto her lap. Jillene wiggles out of her mothers arms, flings herself on the floor, and begins to kick and scream.

WHAT TO TELL THE PARENT   The mother was right in her attempts to limit, distract, and redirect Jillene. The offer of a story and holding her on her lap were positive behaviors. However, because Jillene is struggling with closeness and distance and control of mother, she will likely protest anything that her mother does. Talk with the mother about what Jillene is learning from the ways the mother sets limits.

Children of this age often protest being picked up without warning. Such an action can produce feelings of helplessness and dependence at a time when children are sensitive to these feelings.

DEVELOPMENTAL INFORMATION

At about 20 months, children have some self-awareness. This knowledge both pleases and scares them. They are excited about their independence, but worry that caregivers or parents will no longer be available to help them in times of trouble. Their concerns focus on two issues: **Can I get Mom to come when I need her**? And, **Can I be competent enough to get what I need**? Jillene is working on both issues. She is exploring her ability to make the TV turn on and off (a separation issue with control of starting and stopping, coming and going). She also controls the coming and going (availability and engagement) of the mother.

When adults assert their power over children, it threatens their sense of self and power and they resist or protest by having a temper tantrum. These are not unusual behaviors in children this age, but temper tantrums are difficult to ignore and they are difficult for both child and parent.

WHAT THE PARENT CAN DO   During a temper tantrum the child will most often resist attempts at physical restraint. For her, thrashing about provides the only outlet available at that moment. If the child will not allow the mother to hold her, the mother should sit nearby and intervene only if her child is destructive. Tell Jillene that no matter how angry or frustrated she is, she cannot behave inappropriately. Reassure her that her mother will not leave her. When Jillene calms down, the mother can resume the offer to read the story or to play with a favorite toy. Describe what has happened and affirm that Jillene is now in control again and can resume play. This should be said as an affirmation of Jillene's state of control, and not that the mother is giving permission to act inappropriately. The mother could say something like, "You were pretty angry about the TV. But now it looks like you're okay and in control. Would you like me to read the story now?"

ENDING THE ACTIVITY   The mother can try to find an old radio or appliance that Jillene can play with. If Jillene continues to protest the mother and Jillene can play with the toy radio together.

Paper Collage

The logical consequence of preparation for nuclear war is nuclear war.
- Helen Caldicott

GOAL The child will develop the ability to follow directions and accept limits.

AGE 18 to 36 months

PURPOSE To help children channel impulses in a constructive way. Children will develop fine motor control as they use strips of torn paper to make a collage. They will learn to tear in a controlled and purposeful way.

ACTIVITY When her son tries to tear family papers or magazines, the mother should direct him to his own tearing box. She can also bring the box out for him to play with as an independent activity.

Allow the child to tear paper. When there are enough scraps the parent can help him glue the scraps onto another piece of paper to be labeled with his name. Newspapers and paper grocery bags can be used for this as well as construction paper, oak tag, or poster board. The child and his mother can sing together while doing the activity: "This is the way we tear the paper." The mother can ask her son to tell a story about the collage, or comment on the creation. Post it on the refrigerator with a small magnet.

MORE ACTIVITIES When the child is three years or older, the mother can help her child make creative decisions about how and where to place the torn paper to make attractive designs or objects.

If the activity is being done after expressions of strong or negative feeling, the parent might comment about letting out energy as the paper is being torn.

For older children: gather stones and color designs on them. In the fall children can collect leaves and place them on paper.

Old wallpaper sample books are often free for the asking (or available at a very low cost at decorating stores). These provide an ample assortment of paper in different weights, textures and patterns. The larger sheets can be torn out of the books for easier use by the child. Using torn pieces, help the child make pictures of familiar places such as a house, apartment building, church, or store. Torn pieces can also be used to make "wallpaper people" using different colors and textures for legs, bodies, arms, etc.

Sorting Box

Make an assortment of 4" squares by either tearing or cutting a variety of different materials. Once the squares are made, they can be matched in pairs, used in a memory games, or just to touch with eyes open or eyes closed and talking about the different feel of each. (Assortment: plain paper, construction paper, wallpaper (different weights and textures), foil, waxed paper, fabrics, tissue, and cardboard.)

DEVELOPMENTAL INFORMATION
Toddlers start to explore their environment. They learn about the nature of materials by handling them, manipulating them, and acting on them. They learn what objects can be thrown, bounced, and torn. Toddlers are not doing this to be "bad" or mischievous, or to defy adults. Children are merely acting on objects because they can, and because the objects lend themselves to being acted upon in certain ways (e.g., paper can be torn). Adults can help children by giving them appropriate materials (scrap paper, old magazines) and allowing them to tear or pull them apart. This activity gives children an appropriate outlet for urges and at the same time helps with motor control. It also helps children learn how to put things together again.

81

ENDING THE ACTIVITY Encourage the mother to describe what her child did during the activity, being careful not to impose her own meaning. The descriptions should be objective and highlight the tearing and the pasting actions. ("child's name is tearing the paper......now he is pasting it on the paper, and now he's made a picture, using many different colors.") The mother can comment on her child's effort and introduce the next activity or another collage, while smiling and making eye contact with the child.

SUGGESTED READING
Come Back Hannah!

Marisabina Russo (Greenwillow Books, 2001)

We want our country's use of money
and minds redirected from inventing
ways to destroy one another to
learning how to live together.
- Women's Peace Presence

DEVELOPMENTAL TEACHING

Encourage the mother to give her child a container of scrap paper and old magazines that can be put in a small box such as a shoe box with a lid. Suggest that the mother put her child's name on the box and label it "PAPER FOR TEARING." Explore with the mother her own experiences with making messes when she was young. (Most children played with mud, for example.) Encourage the mother to save newspapers or wrapping and tissue paper to use for this activity. The mother might be concerned that this activity will teach her child to tear good magazines or paper. Redirect the child back to his personal box and tell him that the box is the place to find things to tear. When the child is younger, the mother should be encouraged to keep good magazines and fragile objects out of her child's reach.

Playing with Dough

18-36 mo.

DEVELOPMENTAL INFORMATION
Young children learn about their world by sensory means, touching and feeling objects. Children learn about the nature of objects by manipulating them to see what the objects can do, and what the children can do to them. Sometimes they explore materials in intrusive ways, poking and pounding, for example. Sometimes they explore the extent of their own feelings, and take out angry feelings on people and objects, as in punching and pinching. Children have to be given this opportunity to explore and vent feelings so they can learn about limits: of things, other people, and themselves. This activity provides a safe way for children to manage strong feelings and turn them into a constructive form of exploring the properties of materials.

DEVELOPMENTAL TEACHING
Share the above information with the mother. Ask her to observe her child at play, and notice when the child is showing feelings, especially anger, sadness, or excitement and joy. Focus the mother's attention on ways the child explores, whether it be tentatively or intrusively. Talk about the value of each kind of approach to the world. Discuss with the mother the ways she sees her child expressing emotions. Encourage her to talk with her child about what she sees without putting a value judgment on it. Encourage her to identify ways of redirecting intrusive exploration, and providing outlets for feelings, instead of limiting them.

GOAL   The child will develop the ability to follow directions and accept limits.

AGE   18 to 36 months

PURPOSE   To provide opportunity for parents and children to engage in an enjoyable activity similar to those children might observe parents doing. This activity also provides opportunity for children to channel impulses, and learn to control them.

ACTIVITY   A good way to introduce this activity is for the mother to share dough when she is baking. If that is not possible, the mother and child can make play dough. Commercially made play dough, or clay for preschool children, can be bought. The child can first use the dough without accessories. This provides the opportunity to pound, pull, stretch, and pinch the dough or manipulate it in a variety of ways.

The mother can provide small pieces of cardboard, a cookie sheet, pizza pan, or small tray to provide limits or boundaries for the use of the play dough. She can also provide simple toys the child can use with the dough: cookie cutters, rollers, plastic knives and forks. Small boxes or baking pans can also provide boundaries for using the dough. The mother should avoid making models for her child to copy.

MORE ACTIVITIES   As children get older they will spontaneously begin to mold and name their own creations. This indicates a move to a symbolic level of functioning. The child can also use the dough as props in housekeeping or other types of pretend play.

When a child is having difficulty with impulse control, she can be encouraged to manipulate the dough. Again, providing accessories that give boundaries will be helpful.

To make **Play Dough**, use the following recipe:

> Mix 2 parts flour, 1 part salt, and 1 part water to make a soft but not sticky dough.
> Add food coloring to the water to color the dough and a few drops of oil to keep it soft.
> Store in a covered plastic container.

ENDING THE ACTIVITY   Talk with the child about the activity, the fun she is having, and ways she kept the dough contained. Describe what she did, the fun you had together, and things she made. Let the objects dry and paint them at another time. Ask her to help clean up, and talk about what is going to happen next.

Artists

The world must finally understand that we cannot settle disputes by eliminating human beings.
- Jeannette Rankin

GOAL The child will develop the ability to follow directions and accept limits.

AGE 18 to 36 months

PURPOSE To give children the opportunity to express their feelings in appropriate ways through activities and materials. Playing with materials helps children express strong feelings. As they get older children use symbols to represent experiences, even those that are the source of negative feelings.

ACTIVITY Keep a supply of paper and sturdy crayons (thick stubs) on hand. Keep them where the child can reach them and use them at will. The younger child will have to be supervised to make sure the crayons are used as intended. The child should no longer be mouthing objects when using crayons. If she continues to put them in her mouth, re-direct her to put the crayon on paper. Encourage the child to draw when she shows anger or sadness. The father can suggest, "Draw a sad picture." When the drawing is finished, encourage the child to talk about it. Younger children might pound the crayons, or make heavy marks on the paper. Remember, the goal is not to create an artistic product but simply to channel or re-direct feelings.

If the child is not being destructive and is confining the marks or pounding to the paper, that is all right. If the activity is very intense the father should sit near and touch the child, perhaps rubbing her back or shoulders. The father can hold the child on his lap. Do not insist on these activities when the child is upset. If the child is out of control, holding her gently, talking softly, or rubbing her back might be more appropriate. If the feelings are very intense the child needs the physical support of the father. Holding, rocking, patting will help. Positive physical contact should be given in any case unless it will make matters worse. In this case simply stay near the child.

MORE ACTIVITIES Provide Play Dough (see p. 83 for recipe) or clay for pounding, but do not force the child to pound or make angry marks if she refuses or resists. (See above.)

These materials should be available to the child to use on a regular basis. She can use these to make marks or objects that are representative of her experiences and feelings (joys and pleasures as well as fears, sadness, anger). When the child is able to describe what she made, write it down and post it next to the product.

When an older child talks about her feelings, the father can help her reflect on them and the actions that led to them. This should not be done as moralizing about good or bad but in a way to help the child find alternative ways of behaving.

DEVELOPMENTAL INFORMATION
Young children react with their bodies to their experiences. Their entire bodies show joy, anger, or excitement. Children don't have the words yet to say what they are feeling, and they react immediately. Over the course of the first few years, children gradually learn language, which gives them great freedom from the dictates of the body. Children can express themselves by talking instead of acting. About the same time that children are learning to use words, they are learning to use symbols (one of which is language), and can express thoughts or feelings with an intermediate device. They can make angry marks with crayons or pound an object instead of hitting another child or adult.

85

ENDING THE ACTIVITY   The child may need encouragement to start an art activity. Always help her come to some resolution or reflection. The father can say something like, "You were so angry, but I think drawing that picture really helped. Do you feel better now?" Provide physical affection according to the child's needs (hug, pat, back rub). Mention what happens next.

War is an invention of the human mind.
The human mind can invent peace with justice.

\- Norman Cousins

DEVELOPMENTAL TEACHING
Encourage the father to talk about the times his child showed strong feelings. Problem solve about ways to handle feelings in appropriate ways. Encourage him to use strategies that preserve his child's sense of worth. Children react strongly to techniques that are shaming or humiliating. One child described being shamed is "like being a pocket with all of the wrong things inside". Discourage techniques such as standing in corners or being sent to a place alone. Time out should be used as a last resort, and parents should stay near, but out of eye contact, during the time out. **Time out guidelines: 1 minute for each year; e.g., 2 minutes for 2-year-olds, 3 minutes for 3-year-olds.**

Talk with the father about using activities as an outlet for negative feelings. These techniques help manage the feelings. They also communicate to the child that the parent is an ally in the child's struggle to gain control of her impulses and that he can help her handle the demands of the world around them.

Imitations

*Let there be
peace on earth
and let it begin with me.*
- Jill Jackson and Si Miller

GOAL The child will develop the ability to play, pretend, and to use symbols.

AGE 18 to 36 months

PURPOSE To give children the opportunity to imitate caregiving behavior. This activity also gives the opportunity to talk with parents about the care and nurturing of their children. Use this time to talk about the importance of play and playfulness, including memories of play from their own childhoods.

ACTIVITY Encourage the mother to create a "prop box" which contains some kitchen utensils, plastic plates and cups, and dress up clothes (discarded from family members.) Boxes can be old shoe boxes, discarded packing boxes, or even sturdy paper bags. It helps if the mother pastes pictures of the items on the outside of the storage container. These can be cut from magazines or can be hand drawn. The child can be encouraged to cut or tear the pictures, or older siblings might be able to help draw the pictures. Keep the "prop boxes" handy in the play area if there is room. If there is not enough room they can be stored under the child's bed or crib until they are needed. Bring the boxes out during play time.

The mother can help the child dress up, offering a hat or scarf to start. A toddler might not be interested in putting on clothes. She may show more interest in pretending to cook or feed dolls or animals. The mother can encourage this play by holding toys and modeling some of the behavior, adding comments about the similarity to her own care of the child. She might say, "Oh, you're feeding the baby; that's just how mommy feeds you." Other care routines can be substituted for the feeding statement.

As the child gets older and has good language skills, the mother can encourage her to describe what she is doing. Ask leading questions like, "I wonder what the mommy is doing." The mother can also ask perspective questions such as, "I wonder what that baby is thinking about the food?" Or, she can add a make-believe element, saying for example, "I bet the pizza you are making is really good." Here the child is pretending to cook, an observable behavior; the introduction of the idea of pizza is the make-believe element.

MORE ACTIVITIES As the child gets older, boxes could be developed with props for community helpers (firefighters, doctors, mail carriers, crossing-guards) and heroic and fairy tale figures.

DEVELOPMENTAL INFORMATION
Around 18 months of age children begin to recall images of people and events in their lives. This beginning of object permanence allows children to keep pictures of mother and her caregiving behavior in their mind. They can call up these images when they need comfort and she is not around. Imitative play is one way they can recreate these images by acting out the caregiver behavior they had previously received from her.

Just as children imitate the nurturing they see and experience, so they will imitate other actions including acts of aggression they witness or experience in their own lives and especially what they see on television. This might be time to discuss television monitoring and setting viewing limits.

ENDING THE ACTIVITY   Every activity should have a verbal warning that it is ending. Have the next activity ready and let the child know what that is going to be, saying, "In a few more minutes it will be time for a snack/to go outside/ to read a story/or take a nap." Older children might be more resistant to stopping their play. You might give them a little more time to bring a natural end to it, maybe suggesting, "The baby might be ready for a nap. You can put her to bed, and then you can take your nap too."

Try to make your suggestions fit with the play activity. The play should come from the child's imagination. She may resist the parent's attempt to control the play. Encourage the child to help clean up. Creating a sense of order is helpful in getting a child to move on to another activity.

DEVELOPMENTAL TEACHING
Share the above information with the mother. The Home Visitor can encourage her to save old kitchen utensils, hats, purses and other clothes that can be used for pretend play. She can encourage the mother to make dolls or stuffed animals available. Ask the mother to think about her own early memories of play. Try to elicit the pleasure of play. Expand the discussion to include what can be learned through play and how it helps development.

Let's Talk

DEVELOPMENTAL INFORMATION
Toward the end of the second year children develop the ability to symbolize and use objects to recreate experiences by pretending. At first they use toys that are replicas of real objects, toy telephones for example. They imitate behavior they have observed at home such as parents talking on the phone. Imitating parent behaviors are among the first experiences children play out and pretend. Playing in this fashion allows children to feel more grown-up and competent as they see themselves able to imitate adult behavior. By pretending or recreating home experiences, the children are able to feel the comfort provided by the actual experiences of home. The use of the phone, in particular, helps children keep a sense of connectedness, a link with those persons who are meaningful to them. This activity also gives parents the opportunity to talk with children about separations and other meaningful feelings and events.

DEVELOPMENTAL TEACHING
Share the above information with the mother and encourage her to pretend play with her child. As the child develops language skills and is able to say a few words, have a toy phone available. Simple phones can also be made by stringing cardboard boxes together to make a kind of walkie-talkie. Discuss the ways children pretend at this age. Include the fact that children enjoy talking on the phone, and encourage the mother to allow this with close family members.

GOAL   The child will develop the ability to play, pretend, and to use symbols.

AGE   18 to 36 months

PURPOSE   To provide opportunity for parents and children to represent daily activities using toys. It also provides parents the opportunity to talk with children about meaningful events or the relationship between them.

ACTIVITY   Encourage the mother to become a play partner, pretending to call the child on the phone. The conversations can go in several directions.

Pretend play   The mother can engage in a simple pretend conversation around home events. It could include what the mother or sibling is doing. She can also describe what the child is doing or has done that day.

Here is an example for an older child. Pretend the child is a puppy hiding, or a bear sleeping. Using the toy phone, describe the child's play during the action, saying for example, "Sam is sleeping so quietly and is so still in the cave, just like a bear in winter. It's called hibernating." Then ask the child to talk about his play, using the phone.

Separations   If the mother works, she might talk about their separation, what each did, and how much they missed each other, and how glad they were about the reunion.

Dealing with feelings   Phone conversations are a good way to talk about feelings.

MORE ACTIVITIES   Puppet play, as the child gets older, is a natural extension of conversations. Encourage him to talk with other children or with toy dolls and stuffed animals.

You can encourage the child to draw pictures and label events and his feelings.

Have the child write a letter (dictate to the mother) as a follow-up to a phone conversation with friends or relatives.

ENDING THE ACTIVITY   The mother should comment on the child's growing language ability and his use of language to make and keep connections.

89

Saying Goodbye

Your father and I have tried to teach you that violence brings violence.

It is courageous to love, to care for life because it means constant vigilance against any person, any government which dishonors life. War dishonors life.

- A mother's letter to her son on reaching draft age

GOAL   The child will develop the ability to be a responsive partner and to engage in pro-social behavior.

AGE   12 to 36 months

PURPOSE   To provide opportunity for families to develop rituals and routines that will help children cope with separations and help them feel confident in the parents' return.

ACTIVITY   Some of the routines can include, but are not limited to:

Taking along a favorite toy   A child associates these toys with her mother and can use them for comfort in her absence.

Hugs and kisses   A child can develop rituals by certain types of hugs, or by the order in which she bestows hugs and kisses. The child can call the mother back, or return for one more kiss. She may throw kisses from the doorway or window.

Special waves   The mother and her child can develop their own particular wave for good-bye and use that when they leave each other; high fives can be a sign of greeting, affection, or praise.

Separation games   Games like peek-a-boo, with all of its variations can be used for separation play. Sing songs such as "Where is (child's name)?" pretending to look for the child, and showing surprise when you find her. Talk about what the mother and child will do when the mother returns.

Reunion rituals   Develop a special reunion behavior: handshakes, high fives, a hug, kiss, or wave.

MORE ACTIVITIES   These same rituals or routines can be used for bedtime. The mother can identify books about separation. Goodnight Moon, Are You My Mother?, and Runaway Bunny are among some of the more classic ones. Also try Counting Kisses, Babies, and Again!

ENDING THE ACTIVITY   Tell the child how happy you are to be together, adding a reassuring statement that mother will always return.

DEVELOPMENTAL INFORMATION
During the first years children often resist parents' leaving or have a hard time leaving their parents, even for short separations. At about 18 months of age children realize that parents have a life of their own and children often try to control parents' coming and going. While they may know that parents do return, they worry that they might not be able to manage themselves when they are apart. They worry that parents will forget about them, especially if they have had recent negative experiences with parents, such as being scolded, or even having had "bad" thoughts about parents. Developing rituals around separation gives children some comfort and a feeling of control over separations. Rituals help to reassure children that they can be in control and can control or manage themselves in their parents' absence.

DEVELOPMENTAL TEACHING

Explore how the child behaves when the mother is leaving, and how she supports the child in coping with the separation. Help the mother plan to have some time for the child to engage in separation rituals or routines. Until the age of about four years, a child is still shaky in self-concept, especially about being on her own. Remind the mother that separation reactions are not bad; it shows that her child has a special relationship with her. With repeated separations, if not too long or too frequent, the child will gradually learn she is able to manage without the mother around all of the time. Have the mother talk to her child about what she will be doing while away.

The Runaway Bunny

I watched from the faraway safety of childhood.
- Paulette Bates Alden

GOAL The child will develop the ability to be a responsive partner and engage in pro-social behavior.

AGE 12 to 36 months

PURPOSE To provide the opportunity for parents and babies to engage in an activity that promotes relationships between parent and children that will foster learning. It provides an emotional basis for learning and developing competence around literacy.

STORY THEME

Separation and unconditional love

STORY SYNOPSIS

A mother and her bunny are in their house when the little bunny announces his intent to run away from the mother. She says that if he does that she will run after him. The little bunny then tells his mother that he will become a variety of objects that will allow him to move away. She always counters with a related object that will keep her close. In the end the little bunny decides to stay at home and the mother gives him a carrot.

DISCUSSING THE STORY

There is a board book available. The book is long for a very young baby, but the mother can shorten it by leaving out some of the objects the bunny names. She can draw parallels with events familiar to the child, commenting on the child's leaving and returning, and the mother's own leaving and returning.

DEVELOPMENTAL INFORMATION

As children become more independent during the second and third years they want to do things on their own and they resist limits and directions of others, moving away from their primary care givers. Yet, deep in their hearts is a desire to know that adults are available, and will always be there for them. They test out that availability by pushing away at times and demanding care and attention at others. During the second half of the second year babies use appeal mechanisms and behave in a way to bring caregivers close to them. This struggle with closeness and distance is a necessary one, designed to help children learn that they can act on their own without losing the nurturing care of others.

STORY-RELATED ACTIVITIES

Staying close The mother can dramatize the running away and reunion and make physical contact with a hug or pat during the reunion phases. This is a good way to read the story to an infant.

I would be The mother and older toddler can make a game similar to the one in the story. The mother can ask the toddler to name an object and she can name the counterpart.

The chase This game can be played with a child who can crawl or walk. The mother invites the baby to move away. She then introduces a game of chase, pretending to run after or physically crawling after him. She can then invite him to chase her. They can end the chase with a "catch" of each other and a reunion embrace.

We cook The mother and toddler can prepare a snack together.

Memories The mother can recall special moments together. An older child can be asked to recall his special moments.

Literacy connection   The mother can write stories about the special moments as the child tells them. He can also refer to photos or drawings and describe what was going on. The mother can read the story aloud, leaving out some words for her son to fill in. This is not a test, so the word to be given should be identifiable from the pictures.

PARENT - CHILD ISSUES   A parent sometimes is not available with sufficient consistency to reassure the child that needs will be met. The child might then use indirect appeals (e.g., getting into mischief) that force the parent to notice or pay attention. If this issue is not dealt with, it can become a pattern for interaction. This behavior is called "attention getting". The parent can use this story reading as a time to reassure the child about his feelings of anxiety around separation.

If I could have 3
wishes,
world peace would be
all three.
- Marlia Moore, 8th grader

Index to Activities: 24-36 months

goal 7.	**THE CHILD WILL DEVELOP THE ABILITY TO BE A MUTUALLY RESPONSIVE PARTNER AND ENGAGE IN PRO-SOCIAL BEHAVIOR.**

…I want problem-solving, thinking, empowered, compassionate children who know they live in a global village on a fragile planet.
- Dolores Kirk

GOAL The child will develop a sense of body self and self-regulation.

AGE 24 to 36 months

PURPOSE The purpose of this activity is to get parents talking about a positive aspect of their child's emerging self-development, focusing especially on autonomy. This activity may generate reactions parents might have with the child's increasing struggle for independence.

ACTIVITY Find a time when the mother seems to be enjoying her child. Suggest that she hold him comfortably on her lap. Have the mother look into her child's eyes and talk. The conversation should focus around the child's development during the last few months, his growing independence and competence. The mother might even bring up some of their conflicts and talk about how they worked things out in peaceful ways. Support the mother in using non-physical means of discipline and how to use these as models for her son. For example, "When I get angry, I don't hit you, and I don't want you to hit me/sibling/friend/other."

Help the mother identify the milestones her child has achieved and her reactions to them. These should be shared with the child and the mother can review his growth and development from infancy to the present. Provide contrasts, from being a non-walker or non-talker to being a walker/talker. Continue to focus the discussion on developmental progress and growing competence. If the conversation turns too negative, the mother could also discuss her own personal growth and developing competence as a mother. She could describe how she is different now from when the child was first born, and comment on her changing hopes for the entire family and changes in their family life.

MORE ACTIVITIES Suggest that the parent keep a journal or write this conversation to the child in letter form. If necessary the Home Visitor can write down what is being said, and give it back to the mother for the memory book. Take a photograph of the child every month or so. Paste pictures in the journal or scrapbook, along with the written conversation.

ENDING THE ACTIVITY Help the mother end on a positive note with regard to the child's development. Encourage a comforting touch, pat, or hug.

SAMPLE CONVERSATION Below is a letter one two-year old "wrote" to her mother (the mother actually set the child's words down on paper):

Dear Mommy,
Phia beeps. No. Yep. Chicken and french fries. Dora boots. Benny. It's a Daddy. Tickle. Juice juice. Seesa. Phone. Pony.
Love you!
Phia

DEVELOPMENTAL INFORMATION
There are certain important milestones which occur at the end of the second year that move the child into a more independent position. The child now has language and can keep others available even from a distance. Language begins to serve as a mediator when children and parents talk about what is going on and about the child's feelings (e.g., being left behind by the parents from time to time). During this time children are struggling for control and demonstrate their power and self-awareness by denying others what they have been denied. Toddlers are good at saying "no" and sometimes being non-compliant. They spend as much time trying to manage others as they spend managing themselves. By this age children have developed other symbol systems such as pretend play, which helps with some control struggles as they learn to master power issues through play.

CONTINUED

97

Peace is people talking together with a heart in between them.

- Child, Age 8

DEVELOPMENTAL INFORMATION CONTINUED

Parents generally have strong feelings of their own about the child's struggle for control of self and others. If parents are too controlling children will have doubts about their own competence and hesitate to take initiative because of feelings of inadequacy. They may become rebellious or negative. If parents are too permissive, children worry about their parents' availability to keep them safe and in control. They might act out just to test the parents or they can become afraid to act.

DEVELOPMENTAL TEACHING

This activity will elicit developmental information about the child's emerging abilities, especially those dealing with their sense of self, the ability to act more independently, and their struggles with control. It might also give clues about the parent's feelings concerning the child's non-compliance, resistance, and ambivalence. During this time many parents overlook developing competence and opportunities for learning and just focus on the conflicts brought on by power struggles. Use this time to discuss the mother's concerns around her child's behavior, appropriate discipline techniques, and the difference between punishment and discipline. Discuss the shame and humiliation that might develop when a child is too severely or inappropriately punished.

You really can change the world if you care enough.
- Marian Wright Edelman

GOAL   The child will develop trust through secure attachments and meaningful relationships.

AGE   24 to 36 months

SITUATION   The Home Visitor has been visiting the Williams family and working with Ryan for about two years. Recently they have been talking about ending these visits and Ryan's transition to the neighborhood preschool. Ms. Williams is not working and has been the major caregiver for Ryan from the time of his birth. His younger brother will continue to receive home visits. Recently Ms. Williams has complained that Ryan has become more demanding, insisting that she help him play, clean-up, and do other tasks he normally does on his own.

WHAT TO TELL THE PARENT   Share the above information with the mother. Reassure her that this behavior is usual for children as they experience changes. Tell her that it shows that she has a good relationship with her child. He doesn't want to give up a good thing. Encourage her to expect more of Ryan gradually and to tolerate some of his demands. Help her understand that this behavior will be of short duration if Ryan feels secure in their relationship. Children can't give up what they don't feel they have. When he feels secure that the change will not mean a difference in their relationship he will be more likely to give up his demands.

WHAT THE PARENT CAN DO   Initially, Ms. Williams should try to meet the demands while commenting on the change in behavior. She could say something like, "You really know how to put on your jacket, but I guess it's nice to have someone do it for you once in a while." The easy acceptance of the request will communicate her continued availability so that Ryan might resume doing things on his own. If the request continues, the mother might say something like, "I know you like to have me help you put on your jacket, but next time I think you can do it yourself." She can say this as she helps him. The next time she can remind him, by saying, "Here's your jacket. Today I'll watch you put it on by yourself." The mother communicates her willingness to be helpful, but continues to support Ryan's competence and independence.

The mother can help Ryan do something special for the baby, such as make a toy or decorate a box for baby supplies. She can talk with Ryan about his own babyhood, while looking at photos. Others might be included in these activities and help Ryan make a memory book of things that were special about being a baby. Ryan shouldn't be expected to remember, but he may express some of his fantasies about babyhood, along with perceptions of his mother's relationship with the new baby. The activity can be extended to talk about what the new pre-school experience might be like and to create a transition book, "Things I Will Learn (Do, See.)" Make a collage or memory book of things Ryan might have done as a baby and what he can do now, "Then and Now."

DEVELOPMENTAL INFORMATION
Children at any age might protest giving up a special relationship with adults. In this case, Ryan has recently lost the exclusive care of his mother because of his sibling's birth, and now he will lose the special relationship with the Home Visitor. He might also have some worries about the transition to preschool and what he will be expected to do there.

MORE ACTIVITIES Help children cope with transitions through play. Here are some examples:

Going Places Set up two play spaces, one "house" and the other "school". Use vehicles to move back and forth, and miniature people (can be made) to enable the child to enact activities in each of the places.

Hiding and Finding This variation on hide and seek allows the child to test his mother's availability and what it's like to be on his own.

Special play activities Provide modeling clay, finger paints, or water colors as tools to help build competency.

Practice Visit the new setting. At home, play act some of the activities that happened there.

Talk about feelings Most of these activities provide opportunity to talk about the new experience. Gauge the child's feelings and talk about them directly or indirectly.

Reading Read a book about the first day of school. See book list for Katherine Goes to Nursery School.

No peace lies in the future which is not
hidden in the present instant.
Take peace.
The gloom of the world is but a shadow;
Behind it, yet within reach, is joy.
Take joy.
- Fra Giovani, 1513

24-36 mo.

Hear me!
A single twig breaks,
but the bundle of twigs
is strong.
- Tecumseh

GOAL   The child will develop trust through secure attachments and meaningful relationships.

AGE   24 to 36 months

SITUATION   Hossan just celebrated his second birthday. Recently he has been clinging to his mother, not letting her out of his sight when they are together. He constantly asks her to "Watch me," as he plays and learns new skills. Hossan often asks her, "Is it good?" referring to whatever he is doing. Always a good sleeper, now he resists going to bed and sometimes he gets up crying for her in the middle of the night. He has shown some of this same behavior in child care, tagging after the caregiver and constantly trying to engage her in play with him. Sometimes he resists her attempts to direct or redirect him, often saying, "You aren't my mother." He will also go around the room pointing out objects similar to those he has at home. Both adults are puzzled because he had always been a competent, independent little boy, giving them no trouble.

DEVELOPMENTAL INFORMATION
At the age of two, Hossan has become aware that his mother will not always be around when he needs her. He came to this awareness when he hurt himself a few times while exploring his environment. He may have fallen or confronted a barrier that interfered with what he wanted to do. When his mother was not right there for comfort or help, he realized that sometimes he would have to act on his own. At the same time he's concerned that he might not be able to manage by himself.

DEVELOPMENTAL TEACHING CONTINUED   In his child care setting, Hossan gives some evidence of his growing memory. He remembers his mother and can recall her image more easily. Along with her image, Hossan can also recall her standards and these can be used for comfort. Sometimes he feels that to be loyal to her he should resist whatever is different from what she does. He resists the caregiver because her ways are not those of his mother. And he resists in order to maintain a feeling of control when he's away from his mother. Generally as children realize adults will respond to their wishes they give up some of the need for control and become more compliant.

Finally, Hossan is developing a sense of competence, a necessary step in independent functioning. Getting others to follow his wishes gives a child a great sense of freedom because he can engage in exploration and still be sure that he can get adults to be available when he needs them. It leaves him free from worry about basic needs and he can work on developing play and social skills that reinforce his growing sense of competence. As Hossan sees himself as more skillful he will feel more in control. He can begin to control objects in play rather than trying to control other adults or the relationship he has with them.

DEVELOPMENTAL TEACHING
Hossan has fond memories of those times when his mother was always there to care for him and he tries to recapture some of those early experiences when he had the fantasy that she cared only for him.

He is also learning that he has to listen to the directives of others as he is told what to do, or is sometimes stopped from doing what he wants. He wants to see if he has that same kind of power, making others listen to him, and trying to control their behavior.

When Hossan asks to be watched or about the goodness of his play he wants to be reassured that he is competent. His mother or other caregiver can describe his competence instead of merely saying "Yes" or "Good job". When he wants to be played with, respond as often as possible, or give reasons why it isn't possible. Remember, if Hossan feels his requests are being met he will be more likely to accept the limits set by the adults.

Tearing Paper

There mustn't be any more war. It disturbs too many people.
- French peasant woman

GOAL The child will develop the ability to express feelings in appropriate ways.

AGE 18 to 36 months

PURPOSE This activity will help children manage strong feelings in a safe way. When children are angry and tending to become destructive, parents can give them old newspapers or magazines to tear. This will help children express and modify their feelings.

ACTIVITY Place old magazines and pieces of old newspaper or wrapping paper in a small box labeled with the child's name. Wallpaper and paper bags also can be used. The "slick" advertisement inserts in the daily news are good sources. When the child is angry and begins to behave in an uncontrolled way the mother can redirect her child to the "tearing box." Encourage the mother to include paper that is easy to tear as well as paper that might be more difficult so the child has to exert some effort. Having to work harder helps defuse the anger. The mother should stay near and talk about the angry feelings and the outlet being provided, e.g., "That's really mad paper tearing," or, "You were really angry when you tore that paper." The mother can describe what led to the anger and reinforce limits when appropriate.

The mother should also describe the calming effect of the tearing, and her child's ability to regain control of the angry feelings, comply with the limits, and resume more constructive activity. **Note of Caution:** The mother should not leave her child to tear the paper alone, because that could reinforce the destructive behavior. The verbal descriptions act as a mediator for the child and reflect back what is happening in a way that helps modify behavior. Save the torn paper to be used at another time. When the pieces are small enough they can be used for a torn paper collage.

DEVELOPMENTAL INFORMATION
Toddlers, in their struggle for independence, often run into barriers or come into conflict with limits of their environments. They might become angry and respond by acting out. Because their language is not well enough developed for them to talk about what is wrong, they express their feelings through behavior which can be destructive. This activity helps them express their feelings by acting in a safer, more controlled way. Tearing paper, while giving outlet to the destructive urges, does not harm anyone or anything. It helps the child manage a feeling in an appropriate way. The parent can save the torn paper and use it later for making collages (see Activity p. 81).

MORE ACTIVITIES See **"Paper Collage"**, p. 81.

Fingers Stretch
I stretch my fingers way up high.
Until they almost touch the sky!
(Lift hands and stretch.)
I lay them in my lap you see,
Where they're quiet as can be!
(Fold hands in lap.)

ENDING THE ACTIVITY The mother can describe how this activity helps with the expression of feelings. End with a statement of resolution, and reestablish the relationship with the child.

SUGGESTED BOOKS

My Many Colored Days   Dr. Seuss (Knopf, 1996)

Everywhere Babies   Susan Meyers (Harcourt, 2001)

Come Back, Hannah!   Marisabina Russo (Greenwillow Books, 2001)

All Fall Down   Helen Oxenbury (Simon & Schuster, 1991)

Peekaboo Morning   Rachel Isadora (G.P. Putnam's Sons, 2002)

I Touch   Rachel Isadora (Greenwillow, 1991)

Peace.
The choice of a new generation.
- Matt Bell, 7th Grade

DEVELOPMENTAL TEACHING
Share the above information with the mother and encourage her to keep a supply of old paper or magazines her child can tear. When the child becomes angry and starts to have a temper tantrum, tries to throw objects, or begins to be destructive, the mother can direct her daughter to the paper materials and encourage her to tear the paper or pull the magazine apart. Explore with the mother how she deals with anger and how that relates to her own experiences as a child. This time could also be used to help the mother talk about what happens when she is angry with her child. Discuss appropriate methods for setting limits, while still allowing the child to express her feelings. The discussion could also focus on how the mother feels when her child expresses strong feelings, especially anger, and can explore the relationship between the mother's anger and her child's behavior.

Make it Bite

GOAL The child will develop the ability to express feelings in appropriate ways.

AGE 24 to 48 months

PURPOSE This activity will give children the opportunity to play out some of their more aggressive urges. It helps drain off feelings and gives an outlet for creative expression. It also gives parents the opportunity to make a toy with their child and shows the child that parents are partners and allies when the child feels overwhelmed by strong feelings.

ACTIVITY Using puppets is a good way for a child to act out feelings. The father can create a model for dealing with feelings appropriately when he provides outlets such as these. Because the father and his child are playing together, it gives them a chance to talk about family issues and responses to anger.

Puppets with mouths that open and shut can be made from mittens or old socks. The child can glue on scraps of materials for the eyes, nose, and especially the mouth. The child can practice controlling biting by putting an object in the mouth and pretending to bite, then stopping without biting. Buttons attached to the mouth can represent teeth and make the puppet especially appealing to children who like to use objects to "snap" at people. Jello boxes, or small cereal boxes (individual size), slit half-way down one side, are usable for these puppets.

During this time the father might engage his daughter in a discussion about the kinds of things that make her angry. Encourage the father not to quiz or moralize, but simply to engage in conversation. The father might tell stories about when he felt angry and was able to control himself from acting out.

MORE ACTIVITIES Another way to create puppets is to use small paper bags using the fold as the mouth. Have the child create the face with crayons or other materials.

Give the child several puppets and encourage her to create scenarios which she might dramatize by herself or with others.

The Glad Song (Tune: Twinkle, Twinkle Little Star)
When you're glad you wear a smile,
When you're sad you wear a frown.
And if you're sad I'll be around
To turn that frown upside down!

ENDING THE ACTIVITY Say, "When we're angry it helps to talk about our feelings and what makes us angry, or to use our toys to play act and pretend."

DEVELOPMENTAL INFORMATION
From two to four years of age, children are developing language skills. Their vocabulary and verbal ability grow tremendously during this period. In times of frustration or intense excitement they might not be able to find the words to express strong feelings. Children are impulsive and tend to act before they talk, especially in times of conflict. They hit and even bite to make their anger or frustration known. An important developmental task for this age is to find alternative outlets for this anger, especially when it results in the urge to bite. Puppets with mouths that open and close are useful because they offer a symbolic way to "bite" without hurting anyone. Puppets also encourage language development as the children talk for them. Children can talk about their anger through the puppet, distancing themselves a little from the strong emotions they feel.

SUGGESTED BOOKS

Baby Faces	Margaret Miller (Simon & Schuster, 1998)
Happy Days	Margaret Miller (Simon & Schuster, 1996)
Smile!	Roberta Grobel Intrater (Scholastic, Inc., 1997)
My Many Colored Days	Dr. Seuss (Knopf, 1996)
Everywhere Babies	Susan Meyers (Harcourt , 2001)
On Monday When it Rained	Cherryl Kachenmeister (Houghton Mifflin, 1989)
When Sophie gets Angry	Molly Bang (Blue Sky Press, 1999)
No Biting!	Karen Katz (Grosset & Dunlap, 2002)

DEVELOPMENTAL TEACHING

Encourage the father to talk about how he deals with anger, and whether he is teaching his child positive ways to express negative feelings. A child is very likely to imitate what she sees much more than doing what she's told. If the father loses his temper, yells or hits when he is angry, his child is likely to follow that model. Such behavior also can make the child feel less worthy, and will intensify her tendency to act out or strike out when she is angry.

Develop a plan for dealing with feelings and how to model a positive way to express anger and frustration. Help him accept strong feelings in his child while at the same time helping her handle her expressions of emotion.

Conversations - Now You are Three

*If the family
were a boat,
it would be a canoe
that makes no
progress unless
everyone paddles.*
- Letty Cottin Pogebrin

GOAL	The child will develop a sense of body self and self-regulation.
AGE	36 months
PURPOSE	To get parents talking about a positive aspect of their child's emerging self-development, especially focusing on autonomy. This activity may generate feelings parents might have with the child's increasing struggle for independence, separateness and sense of competence.

ACTIVITY Find a time when the father seems to be enjoying being with his child and suggest that he hold her on his lap. As he speaks to her, the conversation should focus around the child's development during the past year and the change in her emerging competence. Help the father identify the milestones the child has achieved to the present and his reactions to them. Focus on his daughter's growing skill in play, art, music, getting along with others, talking instead of hitting out, and dealing more positively with conflicts. Avoid judgment labels like good and bad. Encourage the father to include things that are pleasing to the child as well as adults. If there are photographs of the child, they can be used for this discussion. Encourage him to share these with his child.

Continue with this review adding feelings about the child's growing competence. It is all right if the father shares some negative reactions as long as the feelings are not expressed with an angry voice. Change the subject if the conversation turns too negative, but make a note of the parent's response. The father could also converse about things he would like his child to know about him. Discuss the father's conversations now and how they have changed since earlier ones. The father might comment on changing dreams, or changes in the family life.

DEVELOPMENTAL INFORMATION
There are certain important milestones that occur at the end of the third year that move children to become more independent and competent. The more children feel confident in their own competence, their ability to make an impact on the environment and to control some of the resources that come their way, the more they are able to act on their own and lessen demands made on adults. Around thirty months, children begin to engage in symbolic play, show some competence with language, and initiate constructive activities, helping them feel a sense of mastery over objects. If children's needs have been consistently met, they are less likely to act in ways that force adults to pay attention to them. They will be able to be creative in play, in demonstrating reciprocity and cooperation in their relationships with adults and other children. Progress will be gradual but by the end of the preschool years these children will be confident, competent persons.

CONTINUED

MORE ACTIVITIES Suggest that the father keep a journal, or write to the child in letter form. If appropriate, the Home Visitor can write down what is being said, and give it back to him for the family's memory book.

Have the father take a photograph of baby every month or so. Have him paste this picture in their journal or scrapbook, along with the letter.

Stretching
I'm stretching very tall. (stretch arms up high)
And now I'm very small. (squat and curl up)
Now so tall... (stand and stretch)
And now a tiny ball. (squat and curl up)

ENDING THE ACTIVITY Help the father end on a positive note with regard to his child's development. Encourage him to give her a comforting touch, pat, or hug.

SUGGESTED BOOKS

Lulu's Busy Day   Carolina Uff (Walker & Co., 2000)

Mama's Little Bears   Nancy Tafuri (Scholastic Press, 2002)

Just Like Daddy   Frank Asch (Simon & Schuster, 1981)

In Between   Sandra Boynton (Simon & Schuster, 1984)

So Big!   (Harper Festival, 2001)

It isn't enough to talk about peace.
One must believe in it.
And it isn't enough to believe in it.
One must work at it.

\- Eleanor Roosevelt

DEVELOPMENTAL INFORMATION CONTINUED

Parents sometimes worry that children are too clingy and push them to become independent. Pushing them might contribute to children's feelings of unworthiness which tends to show up at this age. Encourage parents to tolerate some behavior reminiscent of earlier ages. A gentle show of confidence in the child's ability to master objects and situations will often work best.

DEVELOPMENTAL TEACHING

This activity will elicit developmental information about the child's emerging abilities, especially those around her sense of self and ability to act more independently. It might also give clues concerning the father's feelings about his child's ability to act with intention and independence, and lead him to develop stronger bonds between father and daughter.

Hold Me

*I must be
a peacemaker
in each of my roles:
Christian, mother, wife,
worker, gardener,
citizen, voter.*

- Ruth Rylander

GOAL The child will develop the ability to express feelings in appropriate ways.

AGE 24 to 36 months

SITUATION Hannah, age two years, was playing in the family living room as her mother prepared dinner in the next room. Hannah came into the kitchen and the mother noted that she had taken her shoes off and was walking around in her bare feet. Her mother asked her to get her shoes and she would help her put them on. Hannah refused. The mother insisted and Hannah stood her ground. After a few minutes this battle for control ended in a stand off: Hannah's mother got the shoes and put them on her. Hannah had a temper tantrum, trying to push her mother away. Once the shoes were on, Hannah seemed to calm down. She approached her mother asking to be held. The mother wondered what she should do. She worries that holding Hannah now will just reinforce the resistance.

WHAT THE PARENT CAN DO Assure the mother that this kind of behavior is not unusual for children this age. They want to be independent and act on their own but then they worry that they might have gone too far. They know they are still dependent on parents, see them as powerful, and, most of all, want to please the parents and remain close to them. Tell Hannah's mother that it is important to recognize Hannah's need for independence. She still has to remain available to Hannah and let her know that she will not abandon her because of her feelings or behavior.

Encourage the mother to do some or all of the following:
Find times when Hannah can make decisions about her care, such as selecting clothes to wear.

Allow Hannah to take off her shoes at times when it is appropriate and the mother can praise her for her skill.

Avoid control battles. If the mother wants Hannah to put her shoes on, she might be able to distract her, or make a game of getting her shoes. She might say something like, "I bet I can get them before you can."

If Hannah does have a temper tantrum and wants to reestablish a positive relationship, the mother should cooperate. The mother could acknowledge the strong feelings that went on around control. She could say something like, "We both were pretty mad about the shoes." Add a statement about the current situation saying, "It seems that now you feel a little better about the shoes." She can add her own feeling saying, "I feel pretty good now too." Finally she should invite Hannah to help or stay close.

Sometimes the mother still feels angry and wants to punish the child by pushing her away. **Discourage the mother from doing to the child what the child does to her.** It only reinforces the child's feelings that her mother can abandon her at a time of need.

DEVELOPMENTAL INFORMATION
Two year olds are learning to do things on their own. This ability to explore and try out new skills gives them an increasing sense of competence. But sometimes they go too far in their attempts to be independent. They don't like to be limited or told what to do. Being independent or autonomous gives them a sense of power. Limits make them feel like that power is being taken away. The sense of power helps to build self-esteem while feelings of helplessness diminish their self- esteem.

*People should know
that peace
    is always possible
if we try hard enough.
Us kids have
made friends,
   and we're no different,
  just smaller versions
    of grown-ups.*
    - Samantha Smith

GOAL   The child will develop the ability to express feelings in appropriate ways.

AGE   24 to 36 months

SITUATION   Ms. Pierce is concerned about her 28 month old daughter, Tiffany. Recently Tiffany has become defiant and non-compliant, especially when her mother tells her to get ready for bed. The Home Visitor observed that Tiffany is a pretty competent and engaging little girl. She also noticed that Tiffany hits out from time to time. On one occasion when the mother told Tiffany to pick up her toys, Tiffany said, "No," and when her mother insisted, Tiffany made a kicking motion toward her mother, not touching her. Ms. Pierce then became angry and screamed at her daughter, and threatened dire consequences if Tiffany hit her. Tiffany became sullen and resisted any attempts at interaction or direction about cleaning up. Ms. Pierce sent her to her room, and Tiffany began to cry.

MORE ACTIVITIES   The mother can help the child redirect physical aggression by making mouth puppets, p.105, tearing or cutting paper, p. 103, or playing with clay or play dough, p. 83 as described elsewhere in this document. The mother might also play soothing music, dance slowly while holding her child, or sing a peaceful song, such as:

Peace and Quiet (Full music on p. 157)
Peace and quiet, peace, peace, peace.
Peace and quiet, peace, peace, peace.
Peace and quiet, peace, peace, peace.
We all want peace.
We all want peace.
       copyright 1968, Fred Rogers
       Mister Rogers' Neighborhood

Or say these rhymes with the child:

Two Little Hands
Two little hands go clap, clap, clap.
Two little feet go tap, tap, tap.
One little leap up from the chair,
Two little arms go up in the air.
Two little hands go thump, thump, thump.
Two little feet go jump, jump, jump.
One little body goes round and round,
One little child sits quietly down.

Five Little Monkeys
Five little monkeys,
Jumping on the bed.
One fell off and bumped his head.
Mama called the doctor and the doctor said,
"No more monkeys jumping on the bed!"

DEVELOPMENTAL INFORMATION
Two year olds are increasingly aware of the difference in power between themselves and adults. When two year olds feel out of control, their self-esteem diminishes and they act to get it back. The only way they know how to feel powerful is to do to adults what adults do to them. They may act out their powerlessness: give directives, resist or deny, and control another's actions. So two-year-olds become "no-sayers." This helps them feel more in control and heightens feelings of power. However, it can create an unpleasant situation for parents. The resulting power struggle often leads to relational conflict. **Parents have to rely on their relationship with their children, rather than physical power, to get them to act in compliant and pro-social ways.**

Share the above information with the mother. Assure her that this behavior is to be expected for Tiffany's age and situation. However, the goal is to get Tiffany to cooperate and not to resort to physical aggression as a means of feeling powerful. It might be more helpful to both parent and child if Ms. Pierce ignores the hitting or kicking motions, and keeps her focus on the goal of bedtime, clean-up, or whatever. She can make a simple statement about not using physical aggression, saying, "I can't let you kick/hit/yell at me." She can talk about feelings, and remind her of an upcoming event; for instance, "Let's get ready to read a book, get a snack, etc."

It is important that the mother not use physical punishment as a means of control. If Tiffany loses control the mother can hold her gently, (unless she is being hurtful or destructive) and talk softly but firmly about limits and expectations. The mother can also reassure the child that no harm will be done to her and that the mother will keep the child from harming others. If the child struggles, the mother might have to hold her more tightly, but just enough to keep her from hurting herself and others. She can reassure Tiffany that she will be safe from her own impulses and feelings and from the wrath of others. The mother can give her child suggestions for using language to express her feelings instead of acting out physically.

Reading The Chocolate-Covered Cookie Tantrum or When Sophie Gets Angry - Really, Really Angry can help the mother and child talk about feelings and what to do when angry.

ENDING THE ACTIVITY   The mother can comment on her child's regaining control and, without lecturing, reinforce the peaceful alternatives to physical aggression.

Our life is love and peace and kindness and bearing one with another and forgiving one another and not laying accusations against one another, but...lifting one another up with a tender hand.
- Isaac Pennington

Aim That Ball

GOAL The child will develop the ability to follow directions and accept limits.

AGE 22 to 36 months

PURPOSE This activity provides the opportunity for children to channel impulses into controlled throwing.

DEVELOPMENTAL INFORMATION
During the second and third years children are working to develop a sense of independence. Their need to "do it myself" often brings them into conflict with people and objects in the environment, frustrating their attempts to be in control. At this same time children are developing the ability to control large muscles and take delight in throwing objects. They are able to play simple games of catch, being better throwers than catchers. Controlled throwing offers children an opportunity to channel their impulse to throw wildly while exploring the nature of objects or when feeling angry and frustrated. Games that require children to focus, then throw, not only help with motor development but they also model throwing in appropriate ways. When children are limited from exploring, expressing feelings, or engaging in behavior that is developmentally driven, it can affect their self-esteem. They do not learn to manage the impulse to throw indiscriminately and it will resurface at other times.

ACTIVITY Help the father make light-weight balls from tissue paper or aluminum foil. Simple, light-weight "tossing balls" can also be pairs of rolled up socks. Use small bits of tape to secure the balls and use a large piece of cardboard or poster board to draw a target or a bull's-eye. The father can also use small wastebaskets for this purpose. Outdoors, he can designate a certain spot on the ground or a nearby tree. Let the child practice aiming and throwing the ball at the stated targets. For the very young child, around two years or slightly younger, use a light-weight ball with yarn attached to it. In this case you can eliminate the target and let the child control his throwing and retrieving. Adding a target will give another level of control.

MORE ACTIVITIES As the child gets older, play simple games with balls: sitting on the floor and rolling balls to each other. Short distance catch games, or bouncing balls to each other can also be fun.

Do this finger play:

> Here is a ball (make a circle with thumb and forefinger)
> Here is a base (make a circle with two hands)
> A great big ball I see (make a circle with two arms)
> Are you ready? Can you count them? 1-2-3

Draw a large circle on a piece of newspaper and hang it on a wall, fence, couch or chair. Show the child how to aim the ball. Throw the ball towards a target and get the ball in close proximity to it. They take some pleasure in being able to "hit the bull's-eye".

Make toy clean-up in to a tossing game. Use plastic baskets as containers for plastic blocks, small animal figures, stuffed animals, etc. When it is time to clean up the toys, line up the baskets and make a game of tossing the blocks into the block basket, animals into the animal basket and so on. This kind of constructive tossing can also be used to pick up dirty clothes, paper scraps and sorting laundry.

DEVELOPMENTAL TEACHING
Discuss the many ways the child is showing large motor control: pedaling trikes, rolling balls back and forth, and aiming and throwing objects, particularly balls. Encourage the father to direct his child to controlled throwing instead of punishing him or limiting it altogether. Identify safe places to throw or practice hitting a target.

ENDING THE ACTIVITY Comment to the child about how his ability to hit the target and control the ball has increased. Reinforce the fun you have together when doing this activity. Clean up together and talk about what will happen next.

Baking Cookies

GOAL   The child will develop the ability to follow directions and accept limits.

AGE   24 to 36 months

PURPOSE   To help children follow directions, control impulses to mess, or use messy materials in appropriate ways. This activity will be fun for parents and children and give them an opportunity to share with others.

ACTIVITY   Use a simple recipe for making oatmeal cookies with raisins. Take a recipe card with symbols for the measures and ingredients (picture of eggs, cups, spoons, for example) so her child can have visual cues and an early literacy experience.

MORE ACTIVITIES   The child can serve the cookies to other members of the family. The mother can take a picture of her son during the activity and make a simple sign that says "Cookies".

Patty Cake
Patty cake, patty cake, baker's man,
Bake me a cake just as fast as you can.
Pat it, and roll it, and mark it with a "B",
Put it in the oven for Baby and me!

Provide play dough, cookie cutters, and rolling pin for play.

ENDING THE ACTIVITY   Use the time to talk about nutritional snacks. Praise the child and review the process, going over the recipe card, and making association between the words and the pictures.

DEVELOPMENTAL INFORMATION
Toddlers, in their attempt to become more independent, sometimes become willful and want to exert their will on their environment. At the same time they are learning to adapt their will to the wishes of those around them. They begin to develop the ability to control themselves and to follow directions. Children of this age like to feel grown-up by helping adults with adult activities like dusting and picking up toys. They also are beginning to identify with the nurturing behavior of their caregivers. Many children of this age are being toilet trained and are struggling with impulses to mess.   Experiences with food seem a logical way to help children learn to manage the urges to mess, and learn to do things in an orderly way.

DEVELOPMENTAL TEACHING
Share the above information with the mother and encourage her to include her son in a simple baking activity. Explore with the mother how she helped or enjoyed watching adults bake when she was young, and how she might have pretended to cook herself, using dirt or grass outdoors. Explore the ways she might have been included in a baking activity (rolling a piece of dough, perhaps). Help the mother prepare the recipe on a large piece of cardboard, using symbols of the ingredients to be used in the baking activity.

The human contribution is the essential ingredient. It is only in the giving of oneself to others that we truly live.
- Ethel Percy Andrus

True or False

*A quiet conscience
makes one strong.*
- Anne Frank

GOAL The child will develop the ability to play, pretend, and use symbols.

AGE 24 to 36 months

PURPOSE To provide opportunity to talk with parents about children's development in regard to understanding of real and pretend, and what lying means.

SITUATION Jon is almost three years old. He is very active and likes to tumble about. He is especially fond of playing any type of ball game. His mother recently bought him a new rubber ball. She stores it in the back of the hall closet and he is only allowed to use it when they go outside or to the basement. The other day when she was on the phone, he quietly went into the closet, got the ball, and started to throw it around. It bounced against the wall, knocking a picture off and leaving a mark on the wall. He quickly hid behind the couch. When the mother came back to the room she found him hiding and noticed the picture on the floor. She asked him what had happened. Jon just looked at her. The mother then noticed the ball and realized he had been bouncing it around the room. When she asked him directly if that was so, he shook his head. The mother is worried that Jon is beginning to tell lies.

WHAT THE PARENT CAN DO Parents can help their children remain on the right track to developing honesty by following some of these suggestions:

Avoid asking children direct questions about suspected behavior. At the same time, try not to be accusatory. Say something like, "I wonder how that picture got on the floor." Many two year olds will spontaneously respond, "Me."

Restate the rule that no balls are allowed to be played within the house. If the child insists he didn't do it, say that you think maybe he did. You can add that it's always important to tell what really happened. Help the child find a good "hiding" place where he will keep the ball.

Always be truthful with the child.

DEVELOPMENTAL INFORMATION
Until about four years of age children do not have a good sense of what is real and what is pretend or fantasy. They worry about monsters and other things that go "bump in the night". Their perceptions of reality are a mix of what they know, what they think, and what they feel. That is especially true when children have strong feelings which tend to overshadow the knowing and thinking. Young children engage in magical thinking. They imagine that if they wish hard enough or strongly enough wishes will come true. While most children are obedient most of the time, their urges can sometimes cause them to behave in ways they know are not allowed. They are not very good at stopping themselves from doing something that is forbidden. That is why they need a lot of adult supervision and help in doing the appropriate thing. Words alone do not always work.

DEVELOPMENTAL TEACHING
Share the above information with the mother. Help her recall times when she thought Jon's stories were "cute" and she laughed at them. Children do not always distinguish between harmless and hurtful behavior. Reassure the mother that this behavior is to be expected at this age and it does not mean that Jon will grow up to be dishonest or a liar.

24-36
mo.

*Behold how good
    and pleasant it is
for brothers to
        dwell in unity.*
- Hebrew folk song
based on Psalms 133:1

GOAL The child will develop the ability to be a responsive partner and engage in pro-social behavior.

AGE 24 to 36 months

PURPOSE To provide opportunity to talk with parents about expectations about sharing and other social behavior.

SITUATION Jermaine, age two years, and his older sister Susan, age four, were playing in their bedroom. Jermaine had just gotten a new toy, a shape sorter and was trying to fit the pieces into the shapes. Susan walked over and picked it up. Jermaine started to cry. Susan said, "I just want to look at it," but she walked away with it. Jermaine cried louder. Susan called to her mother, "Jermaine's not sharing." Mom yelled back from the kitchen, "Jermaine, you know we talked about sharing." He continued to cry and went over and grabbed the toy from Susan. Susan left the shape-sorter and began playing with her dolls. Jermaine continued to play with his toy.

WHAT THE PARENT CAN DO The mother can be helpful in this situation by coming in to see what is going on. She can then support Jermaine in keeping the toy and encourage Susan to find something else to do. She might suggest that they work together (sharing the toy) by encouraging Susan to help Jermaine, and encouraging Jermaine to accept help, something a two year old does not always want to do.

WHAT TO TELL THE PARENT Two year olds have a difficult time sharing. Developmentally they are not ready to meet this expectation or challenge. Children should not be pressured to behave when they are not developmentally ready for it. That just makes them feel incompetent and they might become more resistant or misbehave in other ways.

Parents can promote sharing, but not expect that it will happen very much on its own. When it does, they should reinforce the child's spontaneous behavior by labeling it and praising it. If Jermaine gives his toy to Susan, the mother can say, "You shared. How nice," or, "It shows you are learning and growing." Rather than referring to sharing, encourage taking turns by saying, "When Jermaine is through playing, it will be Susan's turn." The mother can promote taking turns by saying, "Another turn, Jermaine, and then it will be Susan's turn," or, "Three more minutes and I will let you know that it will be Susan's turn."

Sometimes it is easier for a child to give up or share a toy if he can hold onto it just a little longer. Say something like, "I'm going to count to ten, and you can keep it while I count. When I get to ten it will be time to give it to (child)."

DEVELOPMENTAL INFORMATION
Sharing is one of the most emotionally charged issues in early childhood settings. Children under four have a particularly hard time sharing because of their development and maturation. It's hard for younger children to think of the other child and acknowledge his or her rights to toys. They also have to deal with the issue of possessions as they work through the value of things they possess and the relationship to their self-esteem.

Tell Me a Story

GOAL The child will develop the ability to be a responsive partner and engage in pro-social behavior.

AGE 24 to 36 months

PURPOSE When children are learning to talk they will often describe what they are doing in a sort of "self-talk". Children of this age also love stories. This activity takes advantage of their interest by encouraging them to talk and to tell their own stories.

ACTIVITY The father should set the model by describing his activities. Refer to the activities listed above for ways to do this with a younger child. As his child develops language and begins to say words, the father can extend the words into sentences. Around two years of age his child will be making up sentences, and the father can extend those into stories.

MORE ACTIVITIES The father can make up his own stories about his childhood, everyday events, or about his child's experiences. Children especially like to hear stories about when they were younger (or babies). Tell these stories in a dramatic fashion, emphasizing the issue facing his child (obstacle or success). The same can be true of the father's stories about himself.

The father can sing simple songs, making them up. At times, such as bedtime or naptime he can sing a song written by Fred Rogers about peace and quiet, using those two words over and over again.

> **Peace and Quiet** (Full music on p. 157)
> Peace and quiet, peace, peace, peace.
> Peace and quiet, peace, peace, peace.
> Peace and quiet, peace, peace, peace.
> We all want peace.
> We all want peace.
> > copyright 1968, Fred Rogers,
> > *Mister Rogers' Neighborhood*

Sing Nursery Rhymes and songs that tell a story such as:

Mary Had a Little Lamb
Mary had a little lamb, little lamb, little lamb.
Mary had a little lamb whose fleece was white as snow.
And everywhere that Mary went, that lamb was sure to go.
It followed her to school one day, school one day, school one day.
It followed her to school one day which was against the rules.
It made the children laugh and play to see a lamb at school.

Hickory Dickory Dock
Hickory dickory dock, the mouse ran up the clock.
The clock struck one, and down he ran!
Hickory dickory dock.

DEVELOPMENTAL INFORMATION
During the second year of life children are working to become persons in their own right. They want to do things on their own, sometimes in conflict with parents because of their willfulness. Developing language gives children tools for controlling impulses and substituting words for actions. By telling stories, children gain different perspectives on events as they get reactions and feedback from others. An adult partner is key to the success of language and ones development. The adult becomes the object of language exchanges, and these exchanges heighten the child's awareness of self in relation to others, forming the foundation of social development. Hearing responses to their "stories" prompts children to keep the conversation going. The adult, as a responsive partner, engages the child in a relationship that is mutually satisfying. This relationship fosters the child's desire to please and adapt his or her behavior to the wishes of others.
Children of this age are capable of feeling empathy, or relating to others as though they, themselves, were experiencing events. Stories are good ways to help children focus on feelings of others, whether it is through story or actual experiences.

The Eentsy Weentsy Spider
The eentsy weentsy spider went up the water spout.
Down came the rain and washed the spider out.
Out came the sun and dried up all the rain,
So the eentsy weentsy spider went up the spout again.

Jack and Jill
Jack and Jill went up the hill
To fetch a pail of water.
Jack fell down and broke his crown,
And Jill came tumbling after.

Parents can make up songs to go along with everyday activities by using familiar tunes:

(Tune: Mary Had a Little Lamb)
It's time to put the toys away, toys away, toys away.
Time to put the toys away, and then we'll take a rest

ENDING THE ACTIVITY   The father can say something like, "That was a great song," and show pleasure in the interaction, and then tell his child what is going to happen next.

SUGGESTED BOOK

Babies on the Move   Susan Canizares (Scholastic, Inc.)

DEVELOPMENTAL TEACHING
Encourage the father to talk with his child. As children get older, they will start to say words, and these words can serve as the basis for "stories" or language exchanges. Ask the father how he was talked to as a child. Ask whether anyone in his family loves stories and is a good storyteller. Help the father appreciate the importance of made-up stories of everyday events. Show him how these can be used to create relationships, instill social skills, and expand language development and creativity.

I Want Mom

DEVELOPMENTAL INFORMATION
Devlin might be seeing Sarah as a rival for the mother's availability. For a lot of the time during Sarah's first year, she was probably content to stay put and play with toys given to her. Devlin was probably busy and excited about his own developing ability to explore and manipulate new objects. Through his eyes, Sarah is an intruder, now that she can do what he can do in moving around, although not as skillfully.

Toddlers also have some mixed feelings about growing up, even when there is not a younger baby around. On the one hand they enjoy their freedom and independence and their ability to move away from caregivers. On the other hand they need to know that caregivers will come when they are needed. Toddlers might also have some longings for the "good old days" and the special closeness they had with their mother when they were babies. These feelings might be more intense for Devlin as he sees his younger sister getting some of the good things that he fondly remembers. Her budding independence can interfere with his "specialness" of being independent.

Two year olds are often aggressive. They are good at starting but not at stopping behavior. They are not always aware of boundaries or the effect their actions have on others.

GOAL The child will develop the ability to be a responsive partner and engage in pro-social behavior.

AGE 24 to 30 months

PURPOSE To provide information about sibling rivalry and the form it might take for different ages of children.

SITUATION For the past few months, Devlin, age 32 months, has been more aggressive toward his younger sister Sarah, who is 13 months old. His mother says that some of the time he is really sweet to Sarah, offering her toys when she is upset, and smiling at her attempts to walk. At other times he is mean, trying to take her toys and especially her bottle or pacifier. He has occasionally pushed Sarah away from his play or away from their mother when she is trying to dress or feed her. He seems to show no concern that he might hurt Sarah. The children share a room and a bath, and the mother says she tries to treat them equally, including them both in story and fun times.

WHAT THE PARENT CAN DO Assure the mother that this behavior is to be expected for the age and situation Devlin is in. Add that it is a compliment to her mothering that he wants more of it. Tell her that needs of children are different at different ages. Perhaps the mother could respond to each child a little differently and spend some time with each one alone. She could try some or all of the following:

Compliment or thank Devlin when he is helpful, kind, and sharing with his sister.

Talk with him about what he was like as a baby, and the good times they had together. Be empathic with his feelings of longing for what he has given up. She could say something like, "I think you might be remembering when you were a baby and I fed you." She could add a statement about what she does for him now, in the context of pride in his growing competence. She might say something like, "Now I just cut your food, and you can eat all by yourself."

Tolerate some regression. For example, helping him with something he can already do when he asks.

Let the child know when it is time to move on to another activity, or give up a toy. You can say something like, "Five more minutes, and we'll put the toys away." Try to give enough time so the child can complete anything he has started. Notice when he is almost finished and give another warning of a few minutes; then begin to help the child start to put toys away. Some children respond well to the use of a timer, or a song that might tell about putting toys away (it can be the "Barney Song" or a made-up song).

Review with Devlin the pleasurable times they had together when he was a baby.

WHAT THE PARENT CAN DO CONTINUED

Set a time each day to play with Devlin (like a date). Set a play clock with the hands positioned at the time so Devlin can tell when the time is near for the play activity.

We have not inherited the earth from our ancestors,
we have only borrowed it from our children.

- Anonymous

Being Polite

GOAL   The child will develop the ability to be a responsive partner and engage in pro-social behavior.

AGE   30 to 36 months

SITUATION   Jermaine, age 30 months, had a fight with his mother, Ms. J., over what shoes he would wear. It was raining and Ms. J. told him to take off his sandals and put on his tennis shoes. Jermaine protested slightly, but went on with his morning routine. He ate his breakfast in silence as his mother hurried around getting ready for work. They walked down the street to his caregiver's house. Jermaine refused to let his mother hold his hand and she had to call to him frequently to stay close and not to run ahead. She often had to do this during walks as well. At the caregiver's home Jermaine refused to greet the other children. He stood near the front door, folded his arms across his chest, and with a scowl on his face he lowered his head. Susan and her mother arrived just then. Susan's mother said that she heard that he and his mom were going shopping and that sounded like fun. Jermaine turned his back on her and let out a protest squeal.

WHAT THE PARENT DID   Mrs. J. went to Jermaine. She stooped to put an arm around him, and made eye contact. She said that she thought he might still be angry and disappointed about the shoes. She added that he was angry with her, and that Susan and her mom had nothing to do with it. Mrs. J. told him it would be nice if he could do something about it. Jermaine looked at Susan and her mother and said softly, "Yeah, shopping will be fun." Mrs. J. added, "I guess I was in too much of a hurry to notice how disappointed you were. The next time we will bring the sandals along for play in the house."

WHAT TO TELL THE PARENT   Compliment Mrs. J. for helping to promote politeness instead of rudeness and establishing close physical contact. Reinforce the way she made social and emotional contact by showing empathy and commenting on his feelings without scolding him for having them. She helped him sort out the source of his anger and differentiate between the actual source and those who had nothing to do with his anger and disappointment. Mrs. J. then stated what she expected Jermaine to do, almost as an invitation.

Emphasize that this observant mother helped to promote Jermaine's character development, and she used her relationship with him as a foundation for promoting desirable character traits. At no time did she label his behavior as bad or impolite. In this instance the mother felt confident that Jermaine would do the right thing. Indicate that sometimes she might be a little more direct in her request that Jermaine do the appropriate thing.

DEVELOPMENTAL INFORMATION
Toddlers are caught up in a swell of emotions that color their view of the world and interfere with their reasoning. Sometimes, especially when they are angry, they want to get rid of the emotion, but they don't know how to do so. They have a tendency to give their feelings away, making others angry in turn. Toddlers depend on adults to help them sort out the emotions, by showing them the relationship between actions, feelings, and behavior. They also depend on adults to help them resolve their feelings and end on a positive note.

"difficult situations" in parenting

Helping Infants and Toddlers Deal with Death

In considering the meaning of death for infants and toddlers, one has to take into consideration their age and the relationship to the person who died. Infants and toddlers do not understand death or loss, and tend to react as they might to other separations. They will be aware that the person is no longer around. Their peek-a-boo games are one way they use to master the disappearance or absence of persons and objects. They will also sense that something is amiss, and will be sensitive to the emotional state of meaningful persons around them, even taking on the sadness felt by the adults. They need to be comforted along with the significant caregivers in their lives. And even though they are too young to comprehend the loss and mourn completely, it is an event that is stored in their memory and can resurface at a later age. They may have a new reaction at that time, colored by the developmental stage that they are experiencing.

Many adults think that infants and toddlers are unaware of losses, especially when the loss does not involve the primary caregiver. But in situations such as these, routines are often affected, and the shifts, along with the emotional tone of the caregiver, can bring about changes in the baby's behavior. They may take on the sadness of the mother, or react more strongly and with anger to her absences, which might increase during times like these. Children often regress, losing skills and capabilities they have most recently achieved.

CONTINUED

SITUATION   Shanika, nine months old, is the only child of Mr. And Mrs. Brown. Mrs. Brown's mother died recently at 75 years of age. She had been sick for about three months, and very sick the past two weeks. Mrs. Brown works and Shanika is cared for by a neighbor in the neighbor's home. The grandmother lived nearby and Shanika saw her every week or two. She has not seen her since the hospitalization two weeks ago. Mrs. Brown is quite saddened and has become low key and preoccupied by the death of her mother. Mr. Brown is available for support for both Shanika and her mother. One wonders what Shanika thinks about all of this.

WHAT TO TELL THE PARENT   Here are some tips for parents who might be concerned about the effects of death on infants and toddlers:

Keep the routine as consistent as possible. The ability to predict gives babies a feeling of being in control during times of stress. And consistency in routines serves to reassure the baby that the caregiving will remain constant.

Provide physical contact and comfort. Parent availability is particularly important at times like these. But the parent in this case might be coping with her own grief and may not be fully present with her baby. Another familiar family member or friend can fill that role. And at this age, the baby can use vision and conversation to keep contact with these familiar adults.

Talk to the baby. Talking does more than making contact with the baby. It gives her a sense that mom is trying to explain the changes in feeling that the baby senses and notices. While she may not understand the words, the accompanying affect and tone will provide some comfort. The toddler will be able to understand the words and the mother can say that she feels sad, misses Grammy and that they won't see Grammy anymore. Reading simple stories about animals dying can be helpful.

Be tolerant of the baby's distress signals. This is particularly challenging when the caregiver herself feels so distraught.

Be tolerant of the baby's expression of joy. This is hard because during sadness, the mother might not have the energy to mobilize the spirit to feel the joy the baby is experiencing. Again the mother can turn to another relative or friend to serve this purpose. Reassure her that she need not feel guilty at her difficulty in experiencing the baby's joy, or allowing herself to feel the baby's joy in the midst of her sadness.

When the child is a toddler, the adults can even plan for periods of play to help the child diffuse some of the intense feeling she is struggling with.

If the child is dealing with the death of a parent, it is important to provide consistency in caregiving as much and as soon as possible. Reassure the child that someone will always provide the care; help the child to understand and reassure the child that the parent who died loved her very much and would not have left her deliberately. Empasize that she did nothing to make the death happen or for the parent to die.

It is probably a good idea to revisit the death through stories or pictures at various times in the future to allow the growing child the opportunity to continue to work on the death and bring about full resolution.

Finally, parents often wonder about including young children in any funeral or other types of services. Parents should generally be supported in whatever makes them and the child feel most comfortable. They might want to consider their own religious beliefs, the show of emotion at these events, and the opportunity for the child to feel the physical and emotional availability of the care providing adult.

DEVELOPMENTAL INFORMATION CONTINUED
The baby may cry more, refuse to eat, have digestive upsets, or sleep problems. The more contact or care received from the person who died, the stronger the baby's reactions are likely to be. The death of mothers and other caregivers will bring the most intense distress.

DEVELOPMENTAL TEACHING
Babies' primary concerns are self-centered, revolving around care and availability of the care provider. In the situation cited above, Shanika may sense her mother's unavailability as she deals with her own grief. The unavailability of the mother, not the grandmother's death directly, may result in behavioral distress. She may become sensitive to her mother's distress, and may react to the change in her mother, a behavior she has not seen before. In her own infant way she 'wonders' about the cause and her contribution to the changes, especially the sadness she might notice.

Helping Infants and Toddlers Deal with Divorce

SITUATION   Brian and Angela are parents of two-year-old Chelsea. The parents have been arguing for the past four months, sometimes with loud voices. The mother says that at those times Chelsea covers her ears and hides her head. There is no physical violence with the parents or with Chelsea. The parents have decided to get a divorce. The father has moved out of the home. They ask for help in telling Chelsea about the family break-up.

WHAT TO TELL THE PARENT   Here are some tips for parents who might be concerned about the effects of parent separation and divorce on infants and toddlers:

Tell the toddler what is going on. This information should be given as soon as possible after the parents decide to separate. Both parents should be present if at all possible. The parents can refer to their past conflict and the child's reaction (e.g. covering her ears), and they can interpret that behavior using words like worry, scared, confused.

Reassure the infant and toddler. Parents should reassure the child of their ongoing love for her, that she was not responsible and had nothing to do with the separation, and that it was a problem between the grown-ups.

Maintain consistency in routines. Being able to predict what is going to happen will give the toddler some feeling of control. Make sure children know what is going on when routines change, and who will be caring for them if baby sitters or care-providers change.

Support the child's relationship with the other parent. Unless there are concerns for the child's safety, the parents should provide time to be with the child on a regular basis. If parents can arrange it, some of the time with each parent should be spent in the child's home, especially if that residence has not changed. Parents can maintain contact or keep a communication notebook, photo album or diary that will go with the child so that each parent knows what goes on when they are separated from the child.

Be tolerant of changes in the child's behavior. Give the child time to adjust to the separation. When she acts out, parents can make the link between the events and behavior. Then the parent can offer support and redirect the behavior into more appropriate channels. Don't gloss over changes, and don't try to talk the child out of the feelings, dismiss the feelings, or try to make up for the loss felt by the child.

Support coping strategies. It is important to keep the limits and boundaries and not overwhelm the child with gifts and favors. But it is also important to recognize and reflect the child's attempt at coping. The child will protest the situation. If parents and other adults are not supportive of the coping strategies which might be unpleasant (temper tantrums, for example), the coping behavior might become rigidified into a defense or symptom and become part of the child's character structure.

Share the parents, not the child. If there is shared custody, the parents should work together so the child does not feel as if she were a boarder in someone's house. This might require duplicate possessions and designated space in the homes of both parents.

The emphasis here has been on separation and divorce of parents. However, many of these strategies can be used if parents remarry, or have someone move into their homes, or if non-parental resident adults move out of the home.

DEVELOPMENTAL TEACHING

Infants and toddlers are somewhat self-centered in times of stress. Chelsea will wonder what all of this means for her, what will happen to her, will she still be loved, and what part did she play in the parent separation. In this situation, Chelsea has already shown some reaction to the parent bickering by covering her ears, possibly indicating that it is overwhelming her. The parents can observe her behavior to determine further just what all of this means to her. She might not want to have parents out of her sight, or she may refuse to go with one or the other of her parents. She may show more separation behavior in her play, hiding toys, playing peek-a-boo or hide and seek, or even play out moving or leaving others. Children might show anger at one or the other, or both, of the parents.

Sibling Issues

SITUATION   Emmy Lou, 20 months old, has just become an older sister to twin boys. Her parents have taken care to ensure that her routine and schedule remain consistent and that she has time to spend alone with her parents. In addition, her grandparents spend a great deal of time with Emmy Lou, seeing her several times a week. In spite of all this effort to keep her routines stable, Emmy Lou has begun to have intense temper tantrums. Her mother wonders how she could have prepared Emmy Lou for the changes that would come with the arrival of her siblings and she wonders what else she can do.

WHAT THE PARENT CAN DO   These parents did a lot to prepare Emmy Lou for the big event. It's hard to prepare a child this age because of her level of understanding. She will know something is going on, but even after being told about new babies coming, she probably won't understand until the babies arrive.

Some of the concrete things parents can do when a newborn is expected may include the following:

If the child is old enough, ask what she thinks it will be like after the baby is born. Engage in "what if" situations to see her perspective about how things have changed and what her place will be in the new family group.

Talk about her new role as big sister.

Involve the child in preparations for the new baby. An older child can participate in decisions about baby items such as color or clothes or furnishings.

Prepare a gift that the older child can give to the new baby. Allow her to help with the decision.

Parents may involve an older child in medical events like doctor appointments. Some hospitals offer sibling classes to help prepare the child for the newborn.

BEFORE THE BABY COMES   The parents have already put many strategies into place that should be helpful to Emmy Lou. They need to speak to the conflict that Emmy Lou feels. They can verbalize her struggle over wanting to be independent and struggle to be closely nurtured by parents. Following are additional suggestions:

The parents should continue to spend specific time with her apart from the babies, giving her attention when the twins are sleeping. They can enlist Emmy Lou's aid as an older sister and appeal to the part of her that wants to move forward in her developing independence and confidence. She can be asked to help carry diapering supplies, feeding equipment or toys. She might be able to "entertain" a baby when he is crying. There is nothing like helping a baby stop crying to capture the heart of a sibling.

DEVELOPMENTAL INFORMATION

Toddlers are prone to temper tantrums for a variety of reasons, most of which are developmentally appropriate. In addition to the issues associated with developing autonomy and independence, Emmy Lou is experiencing other typical developmental changes: growth in language and mastering locomotion among others. At the same time, her environment has changed. There are two more people living with her as well as a number who come and go. Finally her role has changed from an only child to a sibling who must share significant people in her life. These are a lot of changes for a twenty-month-old to cope with changes that add stress to her still immature ego.

Another factor Emmy Lou must deal with is her ambivalence about growing up. Her striving for and success with autonomy and independence are gratifying for her. Her sadness at leaving babyhood behind is real, as it is for any child this age. Emmy Lou has the additional struggle of having to witness two babies who are receiving the very nurturing she is reluctant to leave behind. That makes it all the more difficult for her. Her tantrums are a manifestation of her real conflict about leaving behind something good and moving into an uncertain realm.

CONTINUED

The mother can express the pleasure she felt when caring for infant Emmy Lou saying, "You don't remember when you were this little, but I loved holding and feeding you then."

Looking at photos of her mother or father holding Emmy Lou as an infant might also help. The mother can describe the closeness and the pride in Emmy Lou's growing independence by saying, "You seem so proud of yourself when you help me with the babies. You're growing up." She can comment on the emerging relationship between Emmy Lou and the babies.

To acknowledge Emmy Lou's need for attention, make a sign or a pillow that says, "Emmy Lou needs attention." Encourage her to bring this item to her parents when she feels particularly left out.

The mother needs to empathize with Emmy Lou when she wants her mother's attention and cannot have it. Say, "I know you want me to do that for you right now, but I can't. Baby is crying for his dinner and he needs to be fed." This statement gives the baby's perspective and will help Emmy Lou in developing her own empathy for the baby. She has known hunger or sadness and can apply the baby's situation.

Support Emmy Lou's growing independence and progressive development. At this age she might be ready for new friends, activities, or play materials. Arrange for such activities or events.

Assure Emmy Lou of her continuing place in her mother's life. Create a schedule indicating special times alone with her mother, such as sharing a bedtime story or helping with errands.

Involve the child in decisions about the care for the new baby such as selecting what to wear, which blanket to use, or which toy to give the baby.

There are many stories and books about new babies in a family. Read the stories and give the child adequate time to respond.

SUGGESTED READING

Mama's Little Bears   Nancy Tafuri (Scholastic Press, 2002)

Nobody Asked Me if I Wanted a Baby Sister   Martha Alexander (Penguin Putnam Books for Young Readers, 1971)

I Kissed the Baby   Mary Murphy (Candlewick Press, 2003)

When Sophie Gets Angry   Molly Bang (Blue Sky Press, 1999)

The New Baby   Fred Rogers (Putnam, 1996)

DEVELOPMENTAL INFORMATION CONTINUED
In this new environment she is not yet sure that her needs will be satisfied as they were when she was an infant. Her behavior is a good example of the saying "she doesn't know what she wants." She wants to be independent and still be a baby.

134

Temper Tantrums

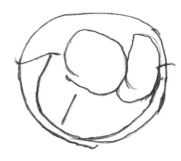

SITUATION Two-year-old LaToya was playing with a puzzle. It was late in the evening and almost bedtime. Her mother told LaToya that soon it would be time to go to bed. LaToya ignored her mother and continued to play. Her mother then took the puzzle away and placed it on the toy shelf. LaToya began to pout and strike out at her mother without making contact. Her mother said, "Don't you hit me." She took LaToya by the hand and pulled her along to the bathroom where the tub was filling with water. The mother turned off the taps and began to remove LaToya's clothes. LaToya lay down on the floor and screamed and kicked her legs so that her mother had difficulty undressing her. Her mother reminded LaToya that she liked to bathe and could just stop screaming and kicking. LaToya continued her tantrum.

WHAT THE PARENT CAN DO Help the parent clarify the issues in this situation and plan different strategies. In this case LaToya's mother could have taken steps that might have averted the conflict.

Give the child warnings when changes are about to occur. The mother might have said that the next event (bath) would follow the ending of the play activity. She could have offered to help bring the play to a successful end by saying, "When you are finished playing with the puzzle, it will be time for your bath. I'll help you put all of the pieces away." Remember that parents are still probably the child's favorite play object.

Emphasize the positive aspect of the next activity. Instead of saying bedtime, focus on an accompanying activity such as the bath, a story, snack, or any activity that the child likes to do with the mother. She could emphasize the "story time together" by saying, "When you finish the puzzle and put it away, we'll get ready for your bath. After the bath we'll have our story time together."

Keep focused on the goal-the bath. Don't be distracted by defiance when it is related to the end of play, not the bath. The issue is the adult control of the ending, so become an ally by stressing the pleasurable activities to come. At this point, ignore that the child is hitting and focus on the bath. Show a little empathy for the child having to stop and give up a play object. Say, "I know you were having fun and don't want to quit, but you like your bath. After your bath we'll read a story and you can pick the one you want me to read."

Remain calm and casual about the hitting, saying "I know you don't want to hurt me. I don't hit you, and I don't want you to hit me. I know you don't like to be told to stop playing, but use words instead of hitting me."

If none of these strategies works and the child continues a tantrum, remain calm. Remember that tantrums have a place in the developmental struggles of children. Tantrums give a sense of boundaries, reassuring children that intense feelings by themselves do no harm. Tantrums also give a sense of equilibrium, showing that strong feelings can be managed and that adults will help when needed.

Talk quietly and hold the child if she tolerates it. If not, sit close by, reassuring the child that you will not abandon her to her emotions or punish her. Tell her you will not interfere unless she or others will not be safe.

Talk about self-control by saying, "You can control your arms/legs/ crying." As the child regains control, recognize that she is managing. Don't talk too much or moralize.

When the tantrum is over, review with the child how she was able to overcome her strong feelings and regain control. Tell her that is a sign of growing up. Reassure her that even when children grow up, parents are available to them.

Instead of giving in to a tantrum, act as an ally by tolerating strong feelings. Use "time out" as a very last resort. Do not isolate the child but keep them in sight without making eye contact. For instance, a special chair, a step, or an adjacent room with an open door may be designated. The rule of thumb is that "time out" should last one minute for each year of age; examples are two minutes for a two-year old, three minutes for a three-year old, etc.

Allow the child to re-establish a positive and reciprocal relationship with the parent.

Toddler Adoption
(Working Through Feelings of Insecurity)

SITUATION   Nora was born to a Mexican-American mother and was adopted at the age of two by parents with fair skin and blond hair. Nora has had a remarkably smooth transition into her new family. Her foster mother had shown her photos of her adoptive parents during the time prior to the adoption, and talked about her new family in positive ways. Nora's parents often shared the story of Nora's life and how they all came to be family, stressing how joyful it made them feel. However, after several instances, in which other children at the park approached Nora and her mother to ask, "Is that your daughter? And "Why does she have black hair? Did you paint it?", Nora seems to have become alternately more clingy and prone to anger outbursts.

STATEGIES FOR PARENTS   This is a time at which parents may wish to revisit some of the steps they took to initially welcome Nora into the family and repeat them to provide some extra reassurance that her new family is a permanent family that loves her unconditionally. Parents can take some of the following steps:

Be the giver of good things - smiles, lullabies, lap time, stories, favorite healthy foods. Slow down and spend some extra family time together. Limit time with others somewhat. Tell your child often that you love her and be generous with encouragement and hugs. Provide lots of opportunities for low stress, comforting activities like working with playdough, water and sand play, finger painting, and swinging.

Stress the importance of family routines and rituals. Children find it comforting to know what to expect, and rituals build family cohesion. For example, have a pancake night each week followed by a neighborhood walk together. Go to the library each Sunday afternoon. At bedtime, go outdoors to look at the moon, then read a story, and then rub your child's back every night in just that order.

Keep a basket of toys and books in each room of your house so that your child can play nearby as you go about daily household tasks.

Make overt claiming statements. Point out all the ways in which you are similar. Say, "You love books, just like Mommy and Daddy." Or "You like to draw with red. Me too! Or "We both love spending time on the glider."

Look at family photos together and narrate the events depicted. Talk about how happy you are as a family.

Read books to your child that depict adoption and multi-cultural families in a positive light. A Mother for Choco by Keiko Kaska, The Family Book by Todd Parr and Loving by Ann Morris are among the many possible choices.

DEVELOPMENTAL INFORMATION
A two-year-old who has experienced toddler adoption is simultaneously dealing with attachment and separation issues, and may well be grieving for the loss of her previous caregiver, all without the benefit of complex verbal language to use in expressing feelings. Latent fears that she may be abandoned by her new family may also be present.

As a child who has experienced toddler adoption does the hard work of re-establishing trust by building attachments to her parents, Nora is probably also having simultaneous urges to experiment with autonomy by resisting requests. An overload of social and emotional tasks may result in developmental delays of about 6 to 12 months. Language skills may regress while anger and tantrums increase.

In addition, children as young as two begin to notice obvious physical differences, especially with respect to skin and hair color, and may feel confused or uncomfortable about such differences.

Make sure that the dolls you choose represent a variety of physical attributes. Buy multiple sets of doll house people as needed to represent your family and those around you.

If your child attends day care or preschool, have her keep a laminated family photo in her cubby. Communicate with caretakers and teachers about your family's values and concerns and ask for support as needed. Make sure everyone in regular contact with your child is familiar with positive adoption language.

Model comfort with adoption as a way of building families by responding to the sincere questions of children and others in a way that educates. When a child asks why your child's hair is black, statements like, "I'm Nora's mommy. She was adopted so she has dark hair like her birth mom." "Adoption is one way people make families" can be a template that a child who was adopted may use later as she responds to adoption questions independently. Empower your child to set privacy limits by modeling responses such as, "That's a private family matter," when someone seems to be asking just out of idle curiosity.

War, Terrorism, Violence

SITUATION This country has recently engaged in a war in a Middle Eastern country. There is a lot about the war in the news, and Ms. Williams is worried that her thirty-month-old son might be affected. Ms. Williams feels fairly calm about the situation, and no one she knows is directly affected by the war. She has been reading about how children might be affected. She has not read anything about children under three years of age, so she assumes that her son might not realize what is going on. She has not changed any schedules and allows the child to watch the news on TV while she prepares dinner.

WHAT TO TELL THE PARENT Here are tips for parents who might be concerned about the effects of war and violence on young children:

Monitor TV viewing and conversations. Parents should be aware of what they are saying around a young child. Children take in and understand more than adults realize. Hushed tones can also create curiosity and anxiety in a young child.

Take care that newspapers and magazines that carry disturbing pictures are not placed where the child can see them.

Don't assume that children don't know what happened. A child is very aware of many things, even when we don't realize it. Even if he doesn't know the particulars, he will know that something is going on.

Don't assume that it will be over once and for all or that his interest will be limited. A child continues to work on issues, assimilate events and process them. He might revisit these issues at different developmental stages.

Find out what information the child has before you offer any. Give the child opportunities to talk about things. Regular reviews of what he has been watching on TV and what he thinks about it will give the child opportunities to bring up issues once he has become skilled with language.

Give information on a need-to-know basis. As the child asks questions give him straightforward, simple and concrete answers. Don't go onto involved explanations. If the child doesn't have enough language to ask questions, you might wonder aloud for him, keeping it short and simple.

Be aware of your own feelings. You can show emotion but don't lose control or act helpless. If you are showing anger, make sure the child knows it is not directed at him. Say, "I just get angry when I think of them hurting, or trying to hurt, people. But I'm not angry at you." Point out that in spite of anger, you are going on with routines and actions of everyday living. Let your child see your compassion and empathy for those who have been hurt.

DEVELOPMENTAL INFORMATION
Generally, children will take cues from parents and their activities of daily living. Children might not show any signs of the effect of the war if their schedules remain consistent and the parents are calm and are not directly involved with the conflict. In this country, children would probably show no adverse effects if their basic needs are being met. It is essential that they not be bombarded by sights and sounds from TV coverage of war and terror attacks. Flashing lights, loud noises, and rapid speech can startle or over-stimulate children and produce anxiety.

Assure the child you are in control, even if it is at a very concrete and immediate level. The child might be concerned about his parent going into unsafe places, on planes or to work in tall buildings. Say, "Daddy/Mommy wouldn't go on the plane in the building if s/he didn't think it was safe."

Point out helpers and caring attitudes (compassion). Talk about people who help: police, firefighters, medical professionals, and government officials, reinforcing the helping roles of those persons.

Find ways for the child to help victims or others in need. If appropriate, the child can save money or toys. Helping at home, preparing food, helping a neighbor or friend can also be useful.

Reassure the child that he is safe and other caregivers are too. Tell the child that you are keeping him safe and that other family members and caregivers are taking measures to be safe.

When a family is called to military service, there will be inevitable anxiety. Acknowledge the worry while assuring the child that you will keep him safe.

Be open and tolerant of his need to communicate. Use story time, bath time and bed time as occasions to share things. Children will generally share concerns. Don't ignore or make light of his feelings. Feelings won't go away just because a child is not allowed to talk about them.

Remember that not all communication is verbal. Consider play, art, reading, or telling stories as means of expression and communication. Use these media to understand a child's concerns and to offer outlets.

DEVELOPMENTAL TEACHING

If parents can keep themselves in control, keep environmental changes to a minimum, stick with routines, keep calm, and offer verbal explanations for changes that do occur, the child might show little or no response to the war or other traumatic event. Changes in the environment, particularly the nurturing environment and caregivers affect children more than war. One exception would be family members being called to military service. When children are separated from significant caregivers, special efforts must be made to minimize disruption of caregiving.

Ms. Williams should not use TV as a distraction without monitoring the contents. Keeping her son near as she prepares dinner, giving him a toy or talking to him may work better. If she must use TV, a calm, age-appropriate video would be preferable.

When Parents Go To Jail

SITUATION Robin, who is one year old, and his two-year-old sister, Molly are living with both parents. However, recently, their father, Mr. Rune, has been sentenced to a half-way house because he was stopped for speeding and the police found marijuana in his car. He will be confined for about a year. Mrs. Rune wonders what she should tell the children and if they should visit him. She turns to her child care expert for some advice. The father has had a good relationship with the children and has participated in their care. The Runes have been fairly happy, although they did argue over his drug use.

WHAT TO TELL THE PARENT Here are some tips for parents who might be concerned about how to talk to their young children about a parent's incarceration:

Tell the toddlers what is going on. Help Mrs. Rune think through what she wants to tell the children. Some families will tell their children directly where the parent is. Others might want to just avoid telling the children the parent is in jail. It is important that the children know the parent is not deliberately staying away on his own.

Give simple explanations for why the father is in jail. Sazie, Elizabeth; Ponder, Diane; and Johnson, Juanita (2001) How to Explain Jails and Prisons to Children : A Caregiver's Guide. Oregon Department of Corrections suggests saying simply, "He/she broke the law", adding that laws are rules for grown-ups, and that jail is like a long time-out. Just be sure they understand that they will not go to jail when they are scolded for breaking a rule.

Reassure the toddlers about the parent's continuing love for them, and that it was not the children's behavior that caused the separation.

Maintain consistency in routines to the extent possible. If the parent had provided some of the care, there might be some changes in the children's routine. Tell the children in advance what the changes will be, always reassuring them that the caregiver will be back at the end of the day. Give them time to get used to new care providers or to new environments. Use graphics and photographs to help them make predictions or anticipate future events.

Support the child's relationship with the parent. Unless there are concerns for the child's well being, another caregiver could take the child to visit the parent if it is not too far, or too much of a struggle. Talking on the telephone might be an alternative, as is writing letters and exchanging photographs.

For another example, the mother can talk about the father when she is with the children, reminding them of past times together, and how the father showed his love and his care for them.

DEVELOPMENTAL INFORMATION
Adult decisions concerning children in this situation should consider the age of the child and the relationship with the person who is in jail. In this case, the parent will be absent and the separation will have to be addressed. Children of this age do not understand the circumstance or the reason for the separation, and may not understand what jail means, but they will notice and react to the parent's absence. Their reactions will be similar to those of other separations. Like the children coping with death and divorce they will take some cues from the feelings shown by the parents. They might experience some confusion and fear as they try to make sense of their conflicting feelings and the various directions they take; (for instance, family anger being directed at the parent and at the authorities responsible for the incarceration.)

The children may show their reaction to the separation in changing behavior. They may regress or become more aggressive, become clingy and resist mother's leaving, or reject other caregivers. Or the children might look for a substitute and accept new care providers too easily. They may show anger at either or both parents. Children may have difficulty sleeping, may refuse to eat, or eat excessively, and, if toilet trained, may lose that ability.

Supporting coping strategies. It is important to recognize and reflect the children's attempts at coping. The children will protest the separation, perhaps by acting out. If parents and other adults are not supportive of the coping strategies which might be unpleasant (temper tantrums for example), the coping behavior might become part of the child's character structure.

DEVELOPMENTAL TEACHING

What makes this situation a little different is that in this case the parent will eventually come back home. One of the challenges to the family is to help maintain the parent's place and relationship with the children, especially when it is likely someone else will provide their care. It is disruptive for children when they know parents are around but they cannot have contact with them. At this age, children are self-centered, wanting to see the parent, wondering about the absence, yet not having the language ability to ask the questions or express the confusion that drives the behavior. If they do have the opportunity to visit the parent, they might experience barriers or the environment may be chaotic, or they may even experience searches of their belongings. All of this can be worrisome to the young child who can't always integrate and make sense of these events.

Raising Empathetic Children

SITUATION   Sara Adams, a bright and active two-and-a-half-year-old falls down and scrapes her knee. Her shrill cry brings her mother running to her side. She says, in a subdued and wounded voice, "Oh, you hurt your knee." She rubs the area, lifts the knee to her lips, then says, "I'll get you a band-aid." The mother gets and applies the band-aid. She says, "Mom takes care of her little girl." Sara runs off to get her blankie.

Later that day, Sara and her mother visit a neighbor who has a three-year old, Shele. During their mother-baby play the two girls fight over Sara's Raggedy Ann doll. When the three-year-old prevails, Sara hits her, and Shele cries. Mrs. Adams goes to Sara and says, "The hitting hurts Shele, and you shouldn't hurt others. You can take turns with the doll. That's called sharing."

The next day, Shele and Sara play together again. As Shele runs to retrieve a ball, she falls. She cries and Sara runs over to where Shele sits on the ground. When Mrs. Adams comes out, Sara runs toward the house. Mrs. Adams asks Sara where she is going. Sara says, "Get a band-aid." Mrs. Adams replies, "She doesn't need one. It's just a little bump. But it is kind of you to think of that." Sara, who had been looking somewhat stressed, handed her 'blankie' to Shele. Mrs. Adams said, "Another kind gesture. I'm so proud of you."

DEVELOPMENTAL INFORMATION

In this complex situation, Sara is showing behavior related to several different developmental issues. She shows identification with the mother, the beginning of fantasy play, sympathy for others, and beginning glimmers of empathy. Empathy is defined as an "understanding so intimate that the feelings, thoughts, and motives of one are readily comprehended by another." (The American Heritage Dictionary of the English Language). It's the ability to take the perspective of, and feel with, the other. That's an over-simplified statement for a rather complex concept. On his website, Dr. Lawrence Kutner (www.drkutner.com) adds that empathy is the ability to understand "what you would feel like if you were in another's situation. Developing empathy is not something we were born with, it's not an innate feeling. It's something we learn."

Learning about empathy can start in infancy. It develops out of the care and nurturing that infants receive from their caregivers, especially the care given in times of distress to comfort the baby. When the quality of care is satisfactory to infants, they enter into strong relationships with the provider and, gradually, over time in the preschool years, they want to be like the caregiver. That process of identification is one of the critical elements in the development of empathy.

DEVELOPMENTAL INFORMATION CONTINUED   Another critical element in the development of empathy is that of sympathy. The American Heritage Dictionary of the English Language defines sympathy as "a relationship between people or things in which whatever affects one correspondingly affects the other". Kutner gives a pre-empathy example that approaches sympathy when he describes a baby crying in the newborn nursery. The other babies, upon hearing the cry, begin their own cries. They cry in response to the discomfort they feel at the crying. Later in their development they remember the feeling and even though they, themselves, are free of distress, they engage in sympathy cries. Empathy adds the dimension of **feeling** and **knowing** what would bring comfort for the other infants. Kutner explains toddlers' pre-empathic behavior as they offer a transition object or toy to the crying infant: these are objects that brought comfort to them when they were hurting. Now they connect the feeling of distress with attempts to comfort another person.

A final element, to be discussed here, is that of fantasy. The ability to fantasize gives the preschooler and older children and adults the ability to really put themselves in the other's position, yet distance themselves from merging or fusing with that person. They use mechanisms similar to those used in distinguishing between real and pretend. Preschoolers, then, can begin to offer true comfort, not just that which makes themselves feel better, but that which they can imagine would make another feel better.

WHAT THE PARENT CAN DO Sara's mother supports her daughter's development very well. First of all, she gives good care in these ways:

She immediately responds to needs, the hurt knee, and the conflict with Shele. When children worry about getting their needs met, they are less likely to develop concerns for the needs of others.

She is gentle in her approach to Sara. Research has shown (Cotton, 2004, www.nwrel.org) that children with non-punitive and non-authoritarian mothers are more empathic.

She states expectations clearly. Clear expectations aid in the development of boundaries, and empathic persons have to know personal boundaries, I and not-I in self-development. They have to be able to fantasize and take on the perspective of the other without losing their grounding in reality. If boundaries aren't clear, there might be a tendency to over-identify with the other person.

She identifies Sara as a caring person. She communicates a belief that Sara could be that kind of person, and labels the behavior that makes it so.

Cotton gives these other suggestions for ways adults can facilitate empathic behavior in young children:

Model the behavior you want to see. Remember identification is a powerful force for learning.

Give reasons for why children should behave in an empathic manner. These explanations should be timely, given when the child has hurt, or otherwise caused distress, to another child. The explanation should include ways to make restitution without always having children apologize. They can help fix what they broke, for example.

Talk about feelings with children. Too often adults sluff off children's feelings as "no big deal", or "you'll be all right". While that might be true in the future, the hurts are real at the moment. Children should know they have a right to their feelings and their points of view. Too many cliches and rules diminish them. And remember the strength of modeling.

DEVELOPMENTAL TEACHING
In this situation Sara is showing typical two-year-old behavior. She acts first (taking the toy), based on her own ego-centric view of events, guided by her feelings. She also shows appropriate behavior in her possessiveness of her doll. In children's developing sense of self, they tend to define self by what they have. If made to give up possessions too soon, especially those important and meaningful to them, they feel as though they are giving up part of themselves. Of course adults want to encourage pro-social behavior such as sharing. They can give reminders of the expectation, eventual sharing, without forcing the issue.

Handful

SITUATION Brian, at age 2-and-a-half years, is considered a "handful" by his mother, and his day care teacher. He doesn't seem to be able to settle into play for any length of time. He constantly gets into mischief, often sweeping toys off the shelves or dumping them out of the toy bins. He runs willy nilly into the other children, pushing them out of his way. He gets angry when adults set limits and resists following the simplest rules. Yet at other times he can be heard calling to his mother, "Hold me, hold me". His teachers say that "he just wants attention".

WHAT TO TELL THE PARENT If the caregiver is going to make demands on the child for compliance, she has to make sure that they have a solid relationship. Below are some tips for helping the child move forward in development:

Maintain availability and be responsive to needs at the time they emerge. If the caregiver cannot immediately take action, she should tell that to the child, then follow-up as soon as she is able (e.g., "I know you want juice right now, but I'm in the middle of a chore, feeding the baby, helping another child right now. I will get it just as soon as am through here." Then, after getting the juice, say, "I'm all done with (chore, etc.), and here's your juice". Then praise the child for being able to wait, and do all of this with joy, showing you really wanted to respond and are glad to have the opportunity.

Let the child know you are pleased (and why) when he is being compliant. This should not be done in a controlling fashion, but just letting the child know you notice the compliance (e.g., "you were able to keep the sand in the sandbox. Now you'll have more to play with. It won't go all over the floor").

Set expectations clearly, breaking them into small steps instead of giving large general directions.

Set expectations within the child's capacity to meet them.

Notice and comment on successes. Remind the child how he is growing in competence. (e.g., "You put that jacket on by yourself. You can do lots of things now. You're growing up").

Play with the child, or teach the child to play. Then use play as an outlet for strong feelings, pretending or play acting, instead of acting out. Children will start pretending as early as a year, but really have symbolic capability by age two.

Give the child undivided attention for at least 15-30 minutes each day. Give more time if you can. During this time, follow the child's lead to the extent possible. Set ground rules around constructive behavior.

DEVELOPMENTAL INFORMATION
During the first three years of life, infants and toddlers work on developing a sense of self as independent persons with a will and control over their lives. They accomplish this in relationship to caring, available, and need-meeting adults. At first, when babies have a need, they have a little worry or anxiety about whether or not that need will be met. When mothers meet the need, giving food for instance, the worry goes away and babies learn to trust that they will get the resources that promote development. When need-meeting is inconsistent, the worry continues. Eventually, babies learn to act for themselves to reduce anxiety. Sometimes that means acting to bring the caregiver (mother), by crying for example. As babies grow they develop capacities in addition to crying that they can use. They can use language or make direct physical appeals to get the mother to come to them. When mothers are unavailable, or act in a haphazard or random way, babies feel, more and more, that they have to force the caregiver to come to them and thus make the anxiety go away. The less secure the baby feels about getting needs met (the less trust), the more the anxiety, and the more the baby acts willfully in negative ways. He gets into mischief or becomes aggressive toward others.

Show empathy for child's feelings and situations. Then help him extend that model to his interactions with others.

Encourage the use of language to express feelings. Verbalize those feelings for the child when he is not able to do so on his own.

Make connections between the child's experience, feeling, behavior, and the reaction of others. For example, "Every time you can't have a toy, you hurt someone. Sometimes kids feel hurt and want to hurt others. But that just makes other kids mad at you."

All of these tips are designed to construct a helping relationship between the child and parent or other adult. At the same time the adult can remind the child about meeting needs and the pleasure they both get from that. Eventually, the child will have the trust that precedes the ability to regulate his own behavior.

DEVELOPMENTAL TEACHING
Even though Brian is 2 ½ he seems not to have the kind of trust that promotes good relationships and subsequent pro-social behavior. As he develops more independence, he struggles with how much he can assert himself and still have the good will of the caregiver. But dependence isn't very appealing either because he doesn't see his caregiver as available to give him what he needs. In a way he takes charge of his own care by acting out and getting the caregiver to come to him. Adults then label his behavior as "attention getting" and unfortunately, tend to withhold attention, fearing that it will just reinforce the negative behavior.

What it really does is reinforce the child's conviction that he won't get what he needs and he has no choice but to continue the pattern. It works better if the caregiver provides for the needs and tells the child that she is doing so. She can also tell him that there are other ways to communicate his needs.

Separations

SITUATION Monica, 19 months, is visiting her mother at a homeless shelter. The mother has been living there for about two months, and Monica has seen her only occasionally. She has been living with her grandmother who has a good relationship with her daughter and talks about her to Monica. During her visits with her mother, Monica is at first standoffish, sometimes warming up just when it is time to leave. Monica is alternately non-compliant and clingy with her grandmother.

WHAT TO TELL THE PARENT We have listed below some other tips that might help children cope with separations in general:

Maintain a familiar environment. In this case Monica was familiar with the grandmother's home. Bringing a piece of equipment, a pillow, blanket, toys, and transition objects can help make the transition more comfortable for the baby.

Provide or keep consistent routines, bathing and eating at the same times as the child did at home.

Implement rituals such as good night kisses, saying good night to objects (like in the book Goodnight Moon on p. 3).

Talk about the absent parent, reassuring the child that the mother is thinking about her, too. Make connections between the child's behavior and missing the mother. For example, when Monica is resistant the grandmother can say things like, "I know it's hard for you to listen to me when you are so used to your mom." She can then take time to talk about the mother, where she is and why. She might say something similar when Monica is clinging to her. This can be done regardless of the age of the child.

Reassure Monica that the grandmother is the caregiver and will be until her reunion with the mother.

Keep photographs around, especially those that show the child with the mother. Take photos at each visit and refer to these frequently.

Engage in separation games such as peek-a-boo or hiding and finding games. See p. 151 for **Here is a Beehive** and **Where Are the Baby Mice?**

Read stories and sing songs about separation.

If resources are available, the mother can call Monica on the phone, or make tape recordings and send these to Monica.

State expectations that are developmentally realistic for the child.

Prepare Monica for visits with the mother and for what will happen during those visits.

DEVELOPMENTAL INFORMATION

One of the tasks of the first three years is for children to develop a sense of self as separate from the mother (or other primary caregiver). They go through stages from making a secure attachment to moving away and becoming an independent being. To do this they have to feel they have the total availability of the mother, who responds in a sensitive manner, giving them what they need when they need it. During this time babies generally tolerate short separations from mother, especially when they are left with reliable, consistent, and familiar substitute caregivers. Prolonged separations, however, can put development in jeopardy. Some researchers who studied separation observed that children's reactions are influenced by the circumstances, the age of the child, and the relationship with the primary caregiver. They found, not surprisingly, that older children (between two and three years) are more able to deal with the separation directly, talking, and even expressing anger, about the mother's leaving. They are able to remember their mothers and to evoke those memories for comfort. Because they have such vivid memories they experience conflict in their loyalties, and have some difficulty in warming up to the substitute caregiver. But this ability to keep an image of mother in memory helps when they reunite with their mothers.

CONTINUED

Talk about what she might be feeling, and the newness of the circumstances.

Put negative behavior in perspective. Remember that it is a reaction to the loss and not a personal reaction to the caregiver. If children are pushed too soon to adjust, they might take a longer time to accept the situation.

DEVELOPMENTAL INFORMATION CONTINUED

Younger children, those under two years, have more difficulty evoking the memory of their mothers, and become more dependent on the caregiver for comfort and security. They are less able to talk about their mothers directly. They are more ready to accept the substitute caregiver but have more difficulty in re-establishing their relationship with their mothers.

DEVELOPMENTAL TEACHING

In this situation, Monica experienced some inconsistency in care even before her mother's admission to the shelter. And she does not see her mother on a regular basis, mostly due to the rules of the shelter and its distance from the grandmother. These circumstances put Monica at greater risk to negative effects of this separation. However, the grandmother is helping by talking about the mother in her absence.

books for peaceful lifestyles

This is a partial list of books, organized by the same goal used for the activities, that can be used at any time with the children.

Goal	Title	Author	Publisher	Date
Goal 1	Where's Nicky?	Cathryn Falwell	Clarion Books	1991
	Pickle and the Ball	Lynn Breeze	Kingfisher	1998
	Max's Bath	Rosemary Wells	Dial	1985
	Horns to Toes and In Between	Sandra Boynton	Simon & Schuster	1984
	Blink Like an Owl	Kathe Burns	Sterling	1998
	No Diapers for Baby	Denise Lewis Patrick	African American Images	1996
	Just Like Daddy	Frank Asch	Simon & Schuster	1981
	What's Inside?	Duanne Daughtry	Alfred A. Knopf	1984
	Where is Baby's Belly Button?	Karen Katz Little	Simon	2000
	Babies	Lara Holtz, ed	Dorling Kindersley	2002
	Wake Up, Me!	Marnie McGee	Simon & Schuster	2002
	Mama's Little Bears	Nancy Tafuri	Scholastic Press	2002
	Lulu's Busy Day	Caroline Uff	Walker and Company	
	So Big!		Harper Festival	2001
	Toes, Ears and Nose	Karen Katz	Simon & Schuster	2002
Goal 2	Nobody Asked Me if I Wanted a Baby Sister	Martha Alexander	Penguin Putnam Books for Young Readers	1971
	The Egg Book	Jack Kent	Mac Millan	1975
	Freight Train	Donald Crews	Scholastic, Inc.	1999
	Duck	Juan Wijngaard	Crown	1991
	What Can You Do in the Snow?	Anna Grossnickle Hines	Greenwillow	1999
	Clap Hands	Helen Oxenbury	Aladdin Books	1987
	Little Goat Sees	Hargrave Hands	Putnam	1985
	Usborne Big Machine Tractors	Usborne	EDC Publishing	1994
	What Can You Do in the Sun?	Anna Grossnickle Hines	Greenwillow	1999
	How a Baby Grows	Nola Buck	Harper Collins	1998
	Baby High, Baby Low	Stella Blackstone	Barefoot Books	1997
	I Touch	Rachel Isadora	Greenwillow	1991
Goal 3	Daddy & I	Eloise Greenfield	Writers & Readers	1981
	Say Goodnight	Helen Oxenbury	Simon & Schuster	1991
	Good Night, Baby	Clara Vulliamy	Candlewick Press	1996
	Good Night, Lily	Martha Alexander	Candlewick Press *	1993
	On My Own	Miela Ford	Greenwillow	1999
	Mama, Mama	Jean Marzollo	Harper Collins Child Books	1999
	Goodnight Moon	Margaret Wise Brown	Harper Collins Child Books	1977
	Bye-Bye, Babies!	Angela Shelf Medearis	Candlewick Press	1995
	Maybe My Baby	Irene O'Book	Harper Collins Child Books	1998
	Me Too	Susan Winter	DK Publications, Inc.	1993
	On the Day I Was Born	Debbi Chocolate	Scholastic, Inc.	1995

Goal	Title	Author	Publisher	Date
Goal 3 cont'd	ABC, I like Me	Nancy Carlson	Puffin Books	1999
	Peek-a-boo Morning	Rachel Isadora	G.P. Putnam's Sons	2002
	I Kissed the Baby	Mary Murphy	Candlewick Press	2003
	Show Me!	Tom Tracey	Harper Festival	1999
	Babies on the Move	Susan Canizares	Scholastic, Inc.	1998
	Away We Go!	Rebecca Kai Dotlich	Harper Collins	2000
Goal 4	Baby Faces	Margaret Miller	Simon & Schuster	1998
	Happy Days	Margaret Miller	Simon & Schuster	1996
	Smile!	Roberta Grobel Intrater	Scholastic, Inc.	1997
	My Many Colored Days	Dr. Seuss	Knopf	1996
	Everywhere Babies	Susan Meyers	Harcourt	2001
	On Monday When it Rained	Cherryl Kachenmeister	Houghton Mifflin	1989
	When Sophie Gets Angry	Molly Bang	Blue Sky Press	1999
	No Biting!	Karen Katz	Grosset & Dunlap	2002
Goal 5	Zoom City	Thatcher Hurd	Harper Collins	1998
	All Fall Down	Helen Oxenbury	Simon & Schuster	1999
	I Touch	Helen Oxenbury	Greenwillow	1991
	Daniel's Duck	Debbie MacKinnon	Dial Books Youth	1997
	Cathy's Cake	Debbie MacKinnon	Dial Books Youth	1996
	Pickle & the Blanket	Lynn Breeze	Kingfisher Paperbacks	1998
	What Shall We Do With the Boo-Hoo Baby?	Cressida Cowell	Scholastic	2001
	Come Back, Hannah!	Marisabina Russo	Greenwillow Books	2001
Goal 6	Peek-a-Boo, You	Roberta Grobel Intrater	Cartwheel	2002
	Book!	Kristine O'Connell George	Clarion	2001
	Cat's Play	Lisa Campbell Ernst	Viking	2000
Goal 7	Willy's Boot	Martha Alexander	Candlewick Press *	1993
	Grandpa	Debbie Bailey & Susan Huszar	Firefly Books, Ltd.	1994
	Big Friend, Little Friend	Eloise Greenfield	Writers and Readers	1991
	The New Baby	Fred Rogers	Putnam	1996
	Finger Rhymes	Marc Brown	Sutton	1985
	Hand Rhymes	Marc Brown	Puffin	1992
	Again! A Baby Bear Book	John Prater	Barrons	2000
	Counting Kisses	Karen Katz	McElderry / Simon & Schuster	2002

* Out of print. Check your local library.

hand and finger rhymes

Where is Thumbkin?
Where is Thumbkin? (hands behind back)
Where is Thumbkin?
Here I am (right thumb appears in front)
Here I am (left thumb wiggles)
How are you today, sir? (right thumb wiggles)
Very well, I thank you (left thumb wiggles)
Go away (right thumb behind back)
Go away (right thumb behind back)
Repeat with pointer (index finger), tall man (middle finger), ring man (ring finger), small man (little finger)

Head and Shoulders
Head, shoulders (point to head, shoulders, etc.)
Knees and toes, knees and toes
Head, shoulders
Knees and toes, knees and toes
And eyes and ears and mouth and nose
Head, shoulders, knees and toes, knees and toes

Here is a Beehive
Here is a beehive (hands clasped)
Where are the Bees?
Hidden away
Where nobody sees
Watch and you'll see them
Come out of the hive
One, two, three, four, five (hands open, hold up fingers one by one as counting
Bzzzz…all fly away

Where are the Baby Mice?
Where are the baby mice (squeak, squeak, squeak)
I cannot see them (peek, peek, peek)
Here they come from the hole in the wall
One, two, three, four, five – that's all!

Johnny, Johnny, Johnny
Johnny, Johnny, Johnny, Johnny, Whoops, Johnny
Whoops, Johnny, Johnny, Johnny, Johnny
(Point to the child's fingers beginning with the pinkie on the word Johnny.
The Whoops comes between the pointer and the thumb.)

Two Little Bluebirds
Two little bluebirds sitting on the hill:
One named Jack, the other named Jill.
Fly away Jack, fly away Jill.
Come back, Jack, come back, Jill.
(Use index fingers to become Jack and Jill.)

151

Buzz, Buzz, Buzz
Buzz, buzz, buzz
I am a bee
Buzz, buzz, buzz
Do you see me?
Buzz, buzz, buzz
How hungry I am
Buzz, buzz, buzz
You better scram!

Five Little Monkeys
Five little monkeys,
Jumping on the bed.
One fell off and bumped his head.
Mama called the doctor and the doctor said:
"No more monkeys, jumping on the bed!"

Four little monkeys...
Three little monkeys...
Two little monkeys...
One little monkey...
...doctor said: "Put those monkeys right to bed!"

Two Little Hands
Two little hands go clap, clap, clap.
Two little feet go tap, tap, tap.
One little body leaps up from the chair,
Two little arms go up in the air.
Two little hands go thump, thump, thump.
Two little feet go jump, jump, jump.
One little body goes round and round.
One little child sits quietly down.

Stretching
I'm stretching very tall.
(stretch arms up high)
And now I'm very small.
(squat and curl up)
Now so tall...
(stand and stretch)
And now a tiny ball.
(squat and curl up)

I stretch my fingers way up high.
Until they almost touch the sky!
(Lift hands and stretch)
I lay them in my lap, you see,
Where they're quiet as can be!
(Fold hands in lap)

Stretch Up High

Stretch up high, stretch down low.
Raise your arms and off we go!
Circle your arm round and round,
Now do the other
And jump off the ground.

Touch

Touch your nose, touch your chin.
That's the way this game begins.
Touch your eyes, touch your knees.
Now pretend your going to sneeze!

Touch your hair, touch one ear,
Touch your two red lips right here.
Touch your elbows where they bend.
That's the way the touch game ends.

Here is a Ball

Here is a ball (make a circle with thumb and forefinger)
Here is a base (make a circle with two hands)
A great big ball I see (make a circle with two arms)
Are you ready? Can you count them? 1-2-3

This Little Piggy

This little piggy went to market; this little piggy stayed home;
This little piggy had roast beef; this little piggy had none;
(During these two lines, the parent touches the toes in turn, starting with the big toe to the fourth toe.)
And this little piggy went wee, wee, wee, all the way home!
(This is said while the parent touches little toe, then creeps fingers up to baby's shoulder.)

Ride a Horsie

Horsie, horsie, ride along
Hits a bump, whoo, whoo!
Horsie, horsie, ride along
Hits a bump, whoa!

Trot, Trot to Boston

Trot, trot to Boston town
To get a stick of candy.
One for you, and one for me,
And one for Dicky Dandy.

5 Eggs and 5 Eggs

5 eggs and 5 eggs, that makes ten.
Sitting on top is a mother hen.
Cheep, cheep, cheep, what do I see?
Ten yellow chicks as fluffy as can be!

A Butterfly Came

A butterfly came to visit me
First it landed on my knee
Then it tried to taste my toes
And now it's sitting on my nose

Miss Mary Mack

Miss Mary Mack, Mack, Mack
All dressed in black, black, black
With silver buttons, buttons, buttons
All down her back, back, back

She asked her mother, mother, mother
For fifteen cents, cents, cents
To see the elephants, elephants, elephants
Jump the fence, fence, fence

They jumped so high, high, high
They touched the sky, sky, sky
And they didn't get back, back, back
'Til the Fourth of July, ly, ly.

Rub a Dub Dub

Rub a dub dub, three men in a tub, and who do you think they be?
The butcher, the baker, the candlestick maker, and they all went to sea.

Rain. Rain

Rain, rain go away, come again another day.
Little (child's name) wants to play!

Engine, Engine #9

Engine, engine #9
Going down the Chicago line
If the train should jump the track
Will I get my money back?
Yes...no...maybe so...

Riding in a Wagon

Riding in a wagon
Riding in a wagon
Wheels go round and round
Riding in a wagon

Patty Cake

Patty cake, patty cake, baker's man,
Bake me a cake just as fast as you can.
Pat it, and roll it, and mark it with a "B",
Put it in the oven for Baby and me!

songs

This is the Way... (Tune: Mulberry Bush)
This is the way we wash our hands,
Wash our hands, wash our hands.
This is the way we wash our hands,
so early in the mourning.

This is the way we comb our hair...
This is the way we brush our teeth...
This is the way we (add your own activity).

The Glad Song (Tune: Twinkle, Twinkle Little Star)
When you're glad, you wear a smile,
When you're sad, you wear a frown.
And if you're sad, I'll be around
To turn that frown upside down!

Hush! Be Still (Tune: Twinkle, Twinkle Little Star)
Hush! Be still as any mouse,
There's a baby in the house,
Not a dolly, not a toy,
But a laughing, crying boy (girl).

The Wheels on the Bus
The wheels on the bus go round and round,
Round and round, round and round.
The wheels on the bus go round and round,
All through the town.

The people on the bus go bump, bump, bump...
The horn on the bus goes toot, toot, toot...
The wipers on the bus go swish, swish, swish...
The babies on the bus go wah, wah, wah...
The driver on the bus says, move on back...

The Noble Duke of York
The noble Duke of York,
He had ten thousand men.
He led them up the hill,
And then back down again.

And when you're up, you're up.
And when you're down, you're down.
And when you're in between,
You're neither up nor down.

Ring Around the Rosie
Ring around the rosie,
Pocket full of posies,
Ashes, ashes,
We all fall down!

The Socks Go on the Feet (Tune: The Farmer in the Dell)
The socks go on the feet,
The socks go on the feet,
We are having lots of fun,
The socks go on the feet

These Are Your Feet (Tune: The Farmer in the Dell)
These are your feet,
These are your feet,
Hi-ho the derry-oh,
These are your feet.

Peace and Quiet (Full music on the next page)
Peace and quiet, peace, peace, peace.
Peace and quiet, peace, peace, peace.
Peace and quiet, peace, peace, peace.
We all want peace.
We all want peace.

The Eentsy Weentsy Spider
The eentsy weentsy spider went up the water spout.
Down came the rain and washed the spider out.
Out came the sun and dried up all the rain,
So the eentsy weentsy spider went up the spout again.

Jack and Jill
Jack and Jill went up the hill
To fetch a pail of water.
Jack fell down and broke his crown,
And Jill came tumbling after.

Mary Had a Little Lamb
Mary had a little lamb, little lamb, little lamb.
Mary had a little lamb whose fleece was white as snow.
And everywhere that Mary went, that lamb was sure to go.
It followed her to school one day, school one day, school one day.
It followed her to school one day which was against the rules.
It made the children laugh and play to see a lamb at school.

Hickory Dickory Dock
Hickory dickory dock, the mouse ran up the clock.
The clock struck one, and down he ran!
Hickory dickory dock.

Peace and Quiet

Peace Links

Mission Statement

Peace Links is a volunteer movement that strives for a safer world for our children by empowering women to work towards abolishing nuclear weapons, educating children and families in conflict management skills, and linking with women and men worldwide who seek alternatives to war.

Peace Links is a nonprofit organization under section 501 (c)(3). Inquires about the publication should be addressed to Peace Links.

305 Wood Street
Pittsburgh, PA 15222
412.471.0302
412.471.4545 fax
peacelinks@aol.com
www.peacelinks.us

Family Foundations
Early Head Start

Mission Statement

Family Foundations Early Head Start is a program of the University of Pittsburgh Office of Child Development. Its primary purpose is to provide support to enhance positive developmental outcomes for children. The focus is to provide a vehicle through which every young child with the support of their family and community will obtain optimal development. Family Foundations serves and partners with infants/toddlers, their parents, extended family, members and their community to self-assess, identify goals, develop and implement action plans to enhance children's development.

Family Foundations provides home-based services which include activities to promote infant/toddler development, enhance parent-child relationships and support families in reaching self-identified goals. The program has established strong community partnerships to support children and their families. Family Foundations is dedicated to providing quality care and services to infants and toddlers in the Early Head Start communities.

University of Pittsburgh
Office of Child Development
400 N. Lexington Avenue
Pittsburgh, PA 15208
412.244.5366
412.244.4766 fax
http://www.pitt.edu/ocd/

STARTING YOUNG_{sm}
order form

Name:_____

Title:_____

Organization:_____

Address:_____

City:_____ State:_____ Zip:_____

Phone: _____ email:_____

Tax Exempt ID#:_____

YES, Send me_____ copies of **STARTING YOUNG**_{sm}

_____loose-leaf vinyl binder - $35.00 each $_____
     (PA residents add 7% sales tax - $2.45each)
_____bound soft-cover - $14.95 each $_____
     ISBN 0-9765689-0-X
     (PA residents add 7% sales tax- $1.05 each)

Shipping & Handling
up to $40.00   -add $ 5.00
$40.00 - $100.00   -add $10.00
over $100.00   -add $15.00

Sub-Total $_____
Shipping & Handling $_____

PLEASE MAKE CHECKS PAYABLE TO: PEACE LINKS

Credit Card users only   Check one: _____VISA _____Mastercard

Account#: _____ Exp. date: _____

Authorized Signature: _____

Peace Links---305 Wood Street---Pittsburgh, PA 15222---412.471.0302
www. peacelinks.us   peacelinks@aol.com